Written and illustrated by

Marji Stevens

Orange All the Way Through

Copyright @ 2023 by Marji Stevens
Published by Mim's Pickety Press, a division of Embracing Grace
Ministries
P.O. Box 5, Rush, NY 14543

www.marjistevens.com
www.EmbracingGraceMinistries.org

ISBN

Edited by Karen Rode, David Buisch, Robert James Shaver
Cover design by Marji Stevens, and Maria Brockett

DEDICATION

To my Lord and Savior, Jesus Christ
Thank you, Father, for sending Your dear Son, Jesus.
Thank you for inviting me on this journey with You.
Thank you for writing Your story upon my heart.

To my family and friends
Thank you to Karen Rode, David Buisch, Robert James Shaver
and the
Upstate New York Word Weaver's Critique group for their
tireless encouragement
and mentoring along my writing journey.

Thank you to my husband, Bill Stevens, (now with the Lord),
our sons Kyle and Jonathan, and my blessed grandchildren for
filling my life with wonderful stories to share.

And heartfelt thanks to the many friends who have had a
large share in
sending forth this book through their faithful and believing
intercession.

To my readers
This book is now given back to God with the prayer that He
will use it
to bring encouragement, inspiration and joy.

This and *That*

Lord, I lay my *this* and *that*
To rest before Your feet.
Help me to, in faith, dear Lord,
Embrace Your grace so sweet.
Help me start each day with joy
Unhindered by the pull
Of all the *this* and *that* in life
That keeps my plate so full.
Lead me far away from
The abrasion of the law
That wears away each drop of joy
With its corrosive draw.
For *this* and *that* I see in me,
Each weak and anxious flaw,
Will never see a lasting change
Through keeping any law.
For *this* You came to conquer.
For *that* You came and died.
So, in the shadow of Your cross
This child can safely hide.
Please draw me as Your precious one,
To rest upon Your lap,
And place my hope, all trusting,
You'll take care of *this* and *that*.

CONTENTS

INTRODUCTION

Since I Am Writing a Book

My father taught me that almost everything in life is "just another funny story to tell." Jesus was a brilliant story teller. He used stories, or parables from everyday life in order to engage people's attention and help them remember His teachings. Stories create word pictures and scientists have produced a mountain of evidence showing that concepts presented as pictures are more likely to be recalled. [1]

The Lord teaches me through stories and pictures. Sometimes I'll be reading Scripture and an image will come to mind and I'll

---

[1] Carmine Gallo, Talk Like Ted, 213

sketch it in my journal. Often, the illustrations come from my everyday experiences, and the people I meet. I believe the Lord is constantly teaching us, and the setting becomes the backdrop of the stories we tell. These are the truths we hand down to our children. "Hey, kids, remember the time when..." Stories communicate history, and what comes wrapped in a story we seldom forget.

Through the illustration of a carrot, I learned about the transformation of the heart of a believer. God wants to create excellence in us that is the same all-the-way-through. I've shared the truth about God's transforming power to thousands of people using the illustration of a simple carrot. I sincerely hope the stories in this book, off the pages of my life, will inspire you.

How It All Began

Years ago, when I first started writing, my only confidence

lay in the fact that my computer had spell-check. I present to you my wobbly first day as a determined writer ...

As soon as my husband, Bill, and our two sons left for the day, my foray into writing a book began. I had no outline, no plan. I only knew I wanted to write stories from my life. Still in my pajamas, I sat down in front of the computer. *Where to begin?* After a few minutes staring blankly at the computer screen, I figured I needed to spark my creativity by reviewing some old journals. Since we live in a storage-challenged 200-year-old farm house, I've learned to tuck my treasures wherever I can find a spot.

Where are my journals? The longer I searched, the more disheartened I became. Dust mixed with mummified flies, rusted paper clips, and old pennies layered everything. The search also revealed more places that needed to be fixed, sanded and painted. *There's no way I can write in an environment like this!* It seemed the most expedient thing to do (since I am writing a book) is to get out the vacuum and clean while looking for my journals.

My mind kept wandering to what my dream office would look like if money was no issue. Anything would be an improvement. My desk was the headquarters for my growing ministry and had to be crammed in the corner of this combination laundry room, playroom and storage area. The kids brought their dirty laundry downstairs, but it often got thrown on top of my desk two feet away from the laundry basket!

I parked the vacuum and decided to take a break to analyze how I could rearrange the room to give me more space. *Gee … wouldn't it be great if we hired a contractor who could push out the wall near the stationary tubs … put cabinets over there … and … a BIG PICTURE WINDOW… and … What am I thinking? We can't afford that …* That thought triggered another one: *maybe I should have a garage sale. Great idea!*

With bubbling determination, I jumped up and headed for the kitchen cupboards to look for things I could put in the sale.

Eee-gads! These cupboards are a mess!

Until we could remodel, the lower cabinets in this farmhouse only served as storage for seldom used pots and pans, old vases, odd serving dishes and a few unrecognizable turn-of-the-century kitchen gadgets. The cabinets weren't built in, they merely leaned against the wall. Gaps in the foundation opened a doorway for incalculable numbers of mice. It also leaked in so much outside air my bathrobe blew in the breeze when I stood at the kitchen sink.

Horrified, I stared at the casualty-littered war zone that blanketed my bottom cupboards. *What a disgrace! How can I relax and write a book when things are like this?* I determined the most expedient thing to do  (since I am writing a book) is to clean while looking for things to put in the garage sale. I dashed for the vacuum, raced back to the kitchen, and started pulling everything out of the cupboards.

In the middle of emptying and sorting, a good friend called. "Hi! Sure, I can chat for a while … Oh, nothing much … just working on my book."

My friend was having a bad day and needed my full attention. As she poured out her heart, I absentmindedly ran my fingers over the edge of our wall-to-wall bookshelf.

"Eee-gads! What a disgrace!" I yelped, interrupting a tender moment. "No - no, not you … it's my bookshelves. I just discovered gobs and gobs of dust … I'll have to call you back later."

Our conversation ended rather abruptly. Soon I was mired up to my elbows in printed matter. At this point, it seemed the most timely, efficient thing to do (since I am writing a book) was to divide the books … one pile of books to keep, and one pile for the garage sale.

Then I heard the sound of the first school bus roar past the house signaling the boys' bus was soon to arrive.

I glanced up at the clock in total shock. *Where has the day gone? Bill will be home from work soon ... and ... oh no, DINNER?!* I hadn't given supper a single thought and I was still in my pajamas.

I sprinted for the kitchen to get something out of the freezer and blundered head-long into the kitchen project I'd started. Frantically, I crammed everything back into the cupboards, then raced to the bedroom to get dressed. I made a bee-line for the bookshelves, shoved all the books back where they came from, and threw the vacuum in the closet while combing my hair and applying lipstick. Darting back to the kitchen, I stuck the frozen chicken casserole in the oven, stuffed a few soda crackers in my mouth, and dashed to my all-purpose office. I threw the duster in the filing cabinet and sank wearily into my desk chair just as Bill walked through the door.

He dropped his bookbag on the floor and smiled approvingly, "There she is!" he exclaimed. "Working on your book I see."

I got up and followed him into the kitchen, "Well... sort of ... it really wasn't a good day," I sighed, leaning into him for a hug. "I had good intentions, but I got distracted."

Bill maneuvered over to the refrigerator with me still attached. "Distracted? By whom?" he asked.

"By ME, by ... everything around here," I replied, with my face muffled in his shirt. Bill extracted his arm from my grip and reached for an apple. "I spent the entire day getting ready to write ... but, things are so ... Can't we do something about the clutter in the laundry room and maybe build an addition so I have a *real* office?"

"Not now," he said. "I just got home."

"I don't mean *now*!" I bristled. "*When?*"

Bill threw his apple core in the garbage pail. "I think if the Lord's telling you to write, you need to forget *where* you're writing and just *get started*."

I didn't admit it, but he was right. To get my surroundings all organized and perfect the whole family would have to move out!

The boys went outside to ride bikes. I sat down to read my Bible. I randomly opened to the book of Ecclesiastes and one line leaped off the page: "He who regards the wind will not sow, and he who regards the clouds will not reap" (11:4). The Holy Spirit personalized it as I read it again. *"She who regards her surroundings will not write, and she who allows herself to be distracted will not accomplish the goal."*

Then I turned to the Psalms and read, "... teach me Lord, to number my days, so that I may gain a heart of wisdom..." (Psalms 90:12) A reference beside it sent me to Ephesians 5:15-16, "See then that you walk carefully, not as fools, but as wise, redeeming the time ..."

This 200-year-old house would never be perfect. Changes will come in the stretch of time. I will need to learn patience and how to be content in my current circumstances.

I reached for my journal and wrote:

"Waiting for things to be perfect before stepping out will only choke my creativity and waste precious time. Lord, keep me to Your path. I want to be a wise woman who can keep a sunny, simple faith despite what's happening around me. Help me to live in the flow of Your peace, drawing on Your strength to accomplish the things You have me to do."

Bill lumbered downstairs after a brief nap, and I found him peering in the refrigerator. Grabbing the cheese and mustard, he walked over to the counter. "Have you given any thought to dinner?"

"Remember how you told me earlier not to let myself get distracted about *where* I write, but just start writing?"

"Did I say that? Smart fella." Bill lifted the lid from a pan on the stove. Then, he opened the oven door.

"You're right," I said. "The Lord confirmed what you said. I'm getting distracted by my surroundings. Take this old house for example. It creaks out, 'Fix me! Insulate me! Paint me! While the kids cry out, 'Feed me! Drive me! Help me!' Then, of course ..."

Bill interrupted, "How about feed me! I'm starving. Feed me!"

I laughed and handed him the silverware to set the table. The boys scrambled through the door and we sat down to eat. After supper, they did their homework, and Bill and I settled on the couch.

"So, what do you think?" I asked.

"About what?"

"You know ... all I said before ..."

After a thoughtful pause, Bill answered, "In my opinion, you need to slow down, set small goals, complete one task at a time ... and enjoy the day."

I just stared at him. "How do you do that? I download all my confusing thoughts and you sum them up with one compound sentence!"

He patted me on the shoulder as he reached for the remote. "You'll be OK. Trust me." End of conversation.

All the pieces from the day dropped peacefully in place. I cuddled close and put my head on his shoulder. It seemed clear to me, the most expedient thing to do (since I am still writing a book) is to sit by my Honey and relax.

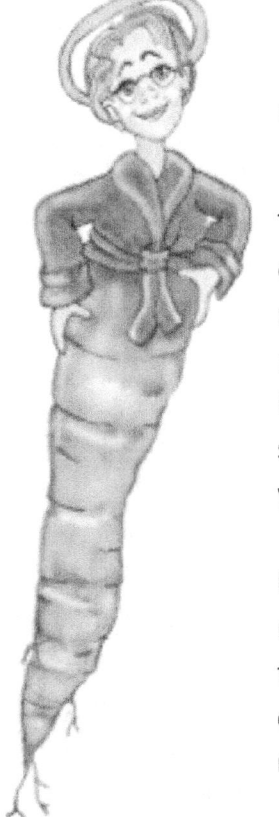

CHAPTER ONE

Orange All the Way Through

The story behind the title of this book originated one day while I pared carrots for the umpteenth time. Pre-sized mini carrots had not yet been invented. So, to eat, was to pare. Between preparing lunches for my kids, snacks, and salads, I figure I've spent close to a year of my life doing this mundane job.

While paring carrots for the dinner salad, I let my thoughts drift to the Scripture verses I'd read that morning. When my focus returned to the task at hand, I realized I'd scraped that carrot totally concave -- all the way down to its middle.

"Phooey!" I mumbled as I stared in disgust at the carrot laying on the sink's edge. Suddenly, I sensed the Lord speaking to me. "Notice the carrot is orange all the way through. It's the same on the inside as it is on the outside. I want you to be like a carrot."

The concave carved veggie rested on the old sink's edge as orange as orange can be — all the way through. I'd never thought about it before; a carrot is not only the same color all the way through, but it's one of the few veggies that also has the same texture and taste on the inside as the outside. I sensed Him saying,

"I'm transforming you into a woman who is all-the-way-through excellent."

The idea of becoming orange-all-the-way-through was a lot to digest in the flurry of preparing dinner. My family never quite understood "sorry, no dinner" because Mom had a revelation to write down in her journal. I whispered a quick prayer that God would help me remember every detail and resumed making the salad.

A Virtuous Woman … Me?

The next morning, during quiet time, the Lord led me to read Proverbs 31. That's the infamous chapter about the virtuous woman. Frankly, I never liked her much. I often skipped that chapter completely. She was THAT woman to me. My competition. My nemesis. It had to be a 'good-hair day' to read about her life. If she's an example of a good Christian woman, then, to quote my kids, I'm in "deep-serious-hot-trouble." There's no contest!

To start with, "She rises while it's yet night…" That doesn't work. I tried getting up before sunrise to pray, but the minute my bedroom door opened the kids were up to join me.

"She does not eat the bread of idleness…" *Great…there goes time in my hammock.*

Not only does she stay up all night, but she also works continuously when she's awake. If I tried living like that, I wouldn't survive long enough to write about it.

"She makes coverings for herself ..." *Now I'm really in trouble.* The last time I sewed something the engine on my sewing machine went up in smoke.

One time Bill mentioned he wanted a floor-length bathrobe to keep his legs warm. I decided to surprise him. I looked for the heaviest velour fabric I could find on sale. It happened to be an ugly gold color, but the price was right. When Bill put it on, he resembled a walking haystack. I'd spent extra time being sure the sash loops were evenly spaced – that was a waste because I found out men don't use loops ... they wing it. I protested when Bill cinched the belt somewhere near his armpits. His reply was, "If it's tied – why fix it?"

The Proverbs 31 woman probably didn't have a closet full of unfinished projects like I do. No way! I can almost hear my mother say, "That Proverbs 31 woman, *SHE* finishes what *SHE* starts." She finished what she started and it's good enough to sell... SO SHE CAN BUY LAND ... not run to the mall.

"She provides food for her household ..." I only like cooking when company comes. The tedium of inventing something every day puts a serious strain on my enthusiasm. Besides, SHE probably has a family who will consume what she prepares without joking about who can remember the number for Poison Control. They probably enjoy leisurely dinners lasting longer than seven minutes and use napkins instead of the front of their T-shirt.

When our youngest son, Jon, was a toddler, he used to wipe his hands in his hair when I wasn't looking. Until almost three, the only hair he had formed a rooster tail up the back of his head. At bath times we'd find bits of the day's meals floating in the water.

I'm sure the homemade bread the notorious Proverb 31 woman made wasn't mistaken for a football, or wedged behind the back wheel of the car to keep it from rolling down the hill. (SHE probably could EAT bread and stay skinny! I bet HER cuticles never saw the inside of a peanut butter jar!)

I slammed the Bible shut. "It's worse than I remember." In my mind, the word "virtue" is translated as perfect and unattainable. I believed becoming a woman of excellence was going to take way more effort than I had the patience for. I felt defeated before I even began. But I'd forgotten the Lord said HE was going to do it.

Embracing Grace

The day rolled on a bit unsteadily. I had so many discouraging thoughts brewing inside me. I needed a pep talk. Bill came home worn out from teaching all day. We got through dinner, the kids' homework, baths, and bedtime. By the time I finished cleaning up the kitchen, Bill was too pooped to even pretend to be interested in my becoming a carrot for God.

Bill fell asleep before I came to bed. I climbed under the covers carrying a cloud of discouragement. On the edge of sleep, an interesting picture formed in my thoughts of a young woman crying into a carefully embroidered cloth. Tiny mirrors sewn on the fabric reflected a broken image of her face. I understood this image was a picture of me crying over the pages of my Bible. *How will I ever measure up and bring You glory, Lord? I can't do it. I try, but I'm never good enough.*

The vision overwhelmed me and I couldn't hold back the tears. I tried to be quiet and not disturb Bill, but he felt me trembling. Normally, if I disturbed him, he'd mumble, "Can't this wait until morning...I have to get some sleep." But this time, he turned over and gently placed his hand on my shoulder. Instantly, I was in a vision again. Bill was no longer the one touching my shoulder.

It was the hand of a voracious lover. In the vision, I turned and folded into His embrace. "What is your name?" I whispered.

His reply washed across me, "My name is GRACE ... embrace My grace."

I understood that by His grace, and only by His grace, would I become a Proverbs 31 woman. It was His work, not mine. He is the answer to all my questions of *how do I change ... how will excellence be formed in me ... how do I get free from bondages and deep furrowed wounds from the past?*

My husband never realized his gentle touch had become the hand of the Lord. Bill's loving response to my tears opened heaven to me. I could see that Proverbs 31 wasn't written to discourage us; it was written to draw us into a deeper dependency upon His Holy Spirit. It's written to show what the fruit of a life hidden in God's embrace looks like. I'd been reading the Word as an assignment rather than an assimilation of His life.

Oh, So Delicious!

The next morning, I cuddled up on the couch with my Bible and a mug of coffee and returned to the study of the virtuous woman. "Her price is above rubies" caught my attention. Why did the Holy Spirit choose rubies? I researched it and found that the ruby is one of 12 stones in the outer vestments of the ancient Hebrew high priest. Each gem was carefully positioned according to God's specific instructions. Gold (which stands for God's love and divinity)[2] made up the settings that held the stones in place right near the priest's heart. Each stone on the breastplate represented one of the 12 tribes of Israel and the blessings ascribed to each. The ruby, which stands for joy, represented the tribe of Judah. When is a ruby the most beautiful? When it is held up to the light. The more the light of Christ shines through our lives the more beautiful we become. The virtuous woman is special only because of the One who shines through her.

That week it was my turn to share in children's Sunday school. I brought a carrot and a paring knife. As I pared the carrot in front of the class, I shared my story. "Why do you think God wants us to be like a carrot?" I asked. Immediately a young boy started waving his hand enthusiastically in the air.

"Oo-oo-oo ... I know," he said breathlessly, then bounced to his feet and declared, "Because He wants us to be delicious!"

The kids laughed, but this young man had said something very profound. "That's a super answer," I said. "When we believe in and follow Jesus, drawing on the strength of the Holy Spirit, He makes us delicious to the Father. He wants to color our lives so we're the same on the inside as we are on the outside, or... orange-*all-the-way-through* just like this carrot."

That young man's name was Raymond. I'll never forget his enthusiastic response to my carrot illustration. When I gave

---

[2] Shari Abbot, The Meaning of Colors in the Bible.
https://reasonsforhopejesus.com/the-meaning-of-colors-in-the-bible/

further study to the word *virtuous*, I came away with the understanding that it's the active quality of excellence. In Hebrew, "virtuous" (*chayil*) means "strength." In the Hebrew culture, a woman of virtue was not considered weak. She was strong, exhibiting the active quality of excellence and strength in every area of her life. Her master, and king, was YHWH alone, and her desire was to be a clear reflection of Him.[3] That lovely yieldedness makes us oh so delicious to God.

---

[3] Her Royal Roots, Huldah David,
http://www.herroyalroots.com/wordstudies/virtuous

Excellence vs Perfection

Excellence is willing to be wrong,

Perfection is being right.

Excellence is risk

Perfection is fear.

Excellence is powerful

Perfection is anger and frustration.

Excellence is spontaneous

Perfection is control.

Excellence is giving

Perfection is taking.

Excellence is confident

Perfection is doubt.

Excellence is flowing

Perfection is pressure.

Excellence is journey

Perfection is destination.

Author Unknown

CHAPTER TWO

Oooh, Honey! Ahhh, Honey!

As God had me on the path to orange-all-the-way-through excellence, there were times when the road seemed to head straight into the muck. The Lord had to remind me *often* to keep trusting and have faith that He would complete the work that He has started. Thankfully, He is not wringing His hands over my life trying to figure out what to do next. He knows right where I am and where I need to go – even when I've lost my footing.

That reminds me of the time my husband allowed me to go fishing with him. He really preferred to go alone. Evidently, I talk too much. I've tried fishing on occasion, but generally, I'm content to set up somewhere on the water's edge to read or write and just enjoy watching the expert experience a great time. My role is to be quiet and say, "Oooh, Honey! Ahhh, Honey," when he lands a fish.

On occasion, I would try my hand at casting, but usually, my line ended up snagged in trees or tangled up like a bird nest. After creating one such bird nest, I went to Bill for help. Without saying a word, he put down his fishing rod, sat on a rock, and began to patiently untangle my mess. His silence was killing me.

"Honey, can I help?" I asked in the sweetest voice I could muster.

"Yup," he replied. "Read a good book."

From that point on I stayed on the shore, mindful that my job was to erupt in praise when he caught one. (I've observed it's OK to make noise at that point.)

The fact that Bill included me in his adventures was always a happy thing. Besides fishing, I've been up in trees, perched in deer stands, and smeared with camouflage paint. I've slept in mouse-infested cabins in the Colorado wilderness, and in the metal cab of our pick-up, I slept in a tent in the Adirondacks when it snowed on the fourth of July! There's just no end to the glamor of wanting to be accepted as one of the guys. The alternative? Stay home.

Big Fish and Grizzly Bears

I remember the time we hiked into the Teton Wilderness "where the fish are big" and the Grizzlies plentiful. When our guide explained what to do if we saw a bear, he couldn't help but see the fear spreading across my face. "Seriously," he said, "don't worry. If you see a Grizzly bear, just drop down on the ground, lie on your stomach, and cup your hands over the back of your neck. You'll be mauled a little bit, but you'll live." Resigned to my fate as a toy for a Grizzly bear's amusement, I settled the knots in my stomach with a chipper, "All righty then ... that's a comfort."

I was surprised when Bill actually encouraged me to fish and even gave me a pair of his chest waders to wear.

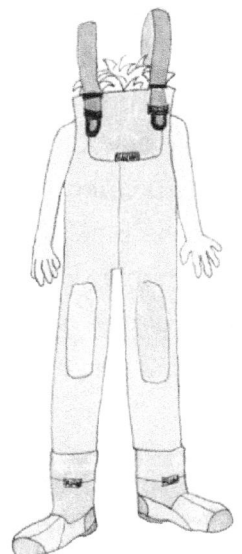

Since Bill is 6'3", and I'm a mere 5'4", pulling the chest waders all the way up, I disappeared except for the top of my head. But being the woman of excellence that I am, I figured he was only trying to protect me. To a bear coming along, he'd take one look at me and think the top half of me had already been eaten! Thankfully, we saw no bears. I lost weight from all the exercise, and Bill caught a fish big enough to feed six adults. (Guess which was my favorite part?)

Then there was the time Bill took me to a fishing spot I'd never been to before. "It's a bit of a walk. We have to cross a *little* potato field and down a *small* hill, but you can handle it," he assured. Well, the *little* field turned out to be three acres, and his *small* hill was more like an Alpine incline.

Bill barreled down the steep slope with practiced ease. "Just grab trees," he yelled over his shoulder. Surprisingly, I did what he said, and it worked. When I got to the bottom he patted me on the back, "You're amazing."

Oh boy …. There's that line. Contain yourself, woman, don't get fancy!" The last time I backpacked down a steep hill I got overconfident and the next thing I knew I was sliding down the mud embankment on my face! That day I learned that just having a backpack doesn't make you a mountain climber!

He kept assuring me it was "just a little bit further," but it turned out to be a path that went underwater. My enthusiasm started to wane back at the Alpine incline, but now my get-up-

and-go was gone! *Warning! Warning!* I heard my conscience scream. *Intense complaining ahead.* My virtuous womanhood was in peril.

I was prepared for a couple hours of shore-sitting that day. My backpack was loaded with boredom survival gear. We didn't have cell phones back then, so to study meant I had to bring the Strong's Exhaustive Concordance, two versions of the Bible, my current notebook, and plenty of pens. To this, I added: a sketch pad, a tarp, a pillow, sunscreen, a raincoat (because we don't leave unless it pours), two oranges, a low-fat candy bar, a high-fat candy bar, gum, and a roll of toilet paper. (Arrgh!)

"This is it!" He announced. "We've arrived."

Mosquitoes and Mud

I surveyed the muddy stream bank with tangled scrub trees. Only a few spring buds dotted the surroundings. It was bleak and thoroughly uninviting to a shore-sitter. Bill wasted no time wading into the water.

My expectations took a nose dive. *I wonder what the virtuous woman would do right about now?* "This is g-r-e-a-t,
Sweetie. I'm so glad I came. I'll set up right here, Honey-bun" ... *On the ground ... In the mud!*

I decided a woman of excellence would make the best of things. After all, we're bonding. That's the important thing— right? Determined to have a good time, I started unloading the contents of my backpack when a chilling realization hit me. NO bug spray!

"Uh ... Marj, I wouldn't set up there if I were you...Look." Bill pointed to the center of the stream. A dark, moving mass slowly moved across the murky water. Hundreds ... no, *thousands* of hideous, voracious, blood-thirsty mosquitoes. The dreaded hatch. The great rite of spring. The first day of their annoying lives, lying in wait for this exact moment. They came. Mobilized for one united action. The feast! An all-you-can-eat feast on white, chubby legs hanging out of *my* shorts.

"I'M OUT OF HERE!" Slapping and dodging for my life, I stuffed everything back into my pack.

"HELP, BILL ... don't just stand there watching me get eaten alive!"

Bill dutifully waded to shore and bent down to pick up my backpack. "Gee, what have you got in this thing anyway?"

"Never mind!" I snapped.

"I've assessed the situation and I think it's too buggy here for you."

"Are you serious right now ... duh."

"You'd better wait in the truck."

Yippee. Saturday in a pick-up truck ... in a potato field ... in the middle of nowhere ... surrounded by blood-lusting mosquitoes!

Grabbing wildly at twigs and grass, and often teetering from my heavy backpack, my attempt to climb the hill was both clumsy and embarrassing. Bill just stepped back and watched the drama. At every advance he'd cheer, "You're incredible!"

At first his words annoyed me, but encouragement can eventually melt the coldest heart.

"You handled that great!" he called from the bottom of the hill. I searched Bill's face for any trace of disapproval and found none.

"Have fun, Honey," I said sheepishly. "Take your time. I'll be fine."

As I sat in the truck picking the dried mud off my knees, I wondered if the virtuous woman would have handled the day any better. Reaching for my Bible, I read, "She comforts, encourages, and does him only good as long as there is life within her" (Proverbs 31:12 Amplified Bible). It also says, "...a woman who reverently and worshipfully fears the Lord, she shall be praised" (Proverbs 31:30). "The heart of her husband trusts in her confidently and relies on and believes in her securely ... her husband boasts of and praises her, saying ... you excel them all" (Proverbs 31:11,28,29).

I thought about how Bill never condemns me—ever. He controls his speech way better than I do. When I tip the scales being grouchy, he'll just look at me and say, "What have you done with my wife?" In that simple statement I hear his encouragement: *This is not like you ... this is not my girl.*

As Bill's red hat appeared over the hill, I finished the day's entry in my journal. "My new backpack is better than I imagined ... went fishing with Bill ... had a *great* time. It's amazing how love deepens in the heart of a woman whose husband nurtures and loves her as Christ loves the church."

Bill seemed a bit surprised to see me smiling and happy. He climbed into the truck, and muttered his famous line: "Yee-uup ... this is what it's all about." Taking a big bite of an apple, he said, "All you need in life is a little time to fish and somebody to help you through the rough spots."

"And plenty of 'Ooo, Honey! Ahhh, Honey ... right, Honey?"

"Yup," he said, reaching over to pat my shoulder. "... and a little bug spray doesn't hurt."

CHAPTER THREE

The Square Christmas Tree

Giant snowflakes fell softly, silently from the gray December sky. The trees stood stripped and poised for winter, and the gardens rested snugly beneath blankets of autumn leaves. As a deep, penetrating cold settled over the valley, the sky darkened and the clouds steadily moved in. This year, for the first time, our boys were given the job of cutting down our Christmas tree. They'd driven out into the back fields on the three-wheeler several hours ago. When the snow began to intensify, I nervously checked the windows hoping they'd make it back before dark.

Soon I heard the sound of their vehicle coming over the hill. I put on my coat and hurried out to meet them.

"MOM! WE GOT IT!" Kyle yelled over the wind. "We got the perfect tree!"

All I could see was a huge snowy heap coated with twigs and weeds being dragged behind the three-wheeler. They cut the engine and triumphantly hoisted up the tree.

"What do you think? Isn't it great?"

The tree was HUGE. It towered over us, defying all pine tree logic, and was absolutely square!

"What's the matter, Mom? Don't you like it?"

Unfortunately, my face had already said it all. "Oh, guys, uh ... it's ... uh ... *square* ... it's ..."

"It's a Snoopy tree!" Jon blurted out. "It needs a home."

Maybe it did need a home, but did it have to be my home? The branches did have pine needles, but they extended out so feebly at the end of the branches, if we tried to prune them into the shape of a Christmas tree, all we'd have left would be sticks.

"Never mind, guys," I said, rising to a more virtuous status. "It's great. We'll fix it up. You did a good job." I don't think they believed me.

Far From Perfect

In the back of my mind, all I could think of were the hours I'd spent creating the *perfect* country ornaments for my *perfect* country tree. Now this *thing,* this gargantuan, dysfunctional pine growth, was about to dominate the entire corner of our living room. Pine needles dropped everywhere as we dragged it through the house. It didn't fit in the living room until we rearranged all the furniture.

I'd found a tree stand at a garage sale over the summer, but it soon became apparent why they were selling it. We heaved the tree back and forth, knocking over lamps and pictures, only to discover the truth—the stand was bent. No matter what we tried, the tree tipped to one side.

I was way beyond the point of grumbling as I looked at it towering in the corner. *My ornaments are going to get lost in all this ugliness.* Maybe stringing the lights in a triangle shape will help. At least at night– if you squint – it *might* resemble a real Christmas tree.

"Is it straight yet?" I bellowed from under the tree.

"It's fine, Mom. Let's get going, our program is almost on."

I had envisioned the three of us blissfully singing Christmas carols as we leisurely trimmed the tree. My boys would stop to hug me. Bill would arrive from work full of energy. He'd sweep me off my feet with jubilant accolades as the tree twinkled brightly in the background. *When will I learn? I bet the virtuous woman wasn't plagued with unrealistic expectations.* Sure enough-- somewhere between hanging the lights and the first line of *Away in The Manger*, I lost the boys.

Moments later, Bill came home. I heard the front door slam and ran to greet him. He let his bookbag drop to the floor, "Before you say anything, I want you to know I'm exhausted. I've discovered no kid wants to learn Social Studies with Christmas vacation around the corner."

"The boys and I put up the Christmas tree. Wait 'til you see it … it's …"

"Oh, thank God," Bill groaned. "I hate that job."

"What I was going to say is it's the homeliest tree I've ever seen … and not only that, remember the stand I bought at that garage sale …"

Bill moaned as he hung up his coat. "Let me get in the house, p-l-e-a-s-e."

The boys heard him come in and came thundering down the stairs. "Dad, Dad, guess what! We got the tree. It's awesome, Dad. You gotta see it."

Bill grabbed a chunk of cheese from the frig. "I can't wait."

"It's huge, Dad; we cut it down way back in the fields. We dragged it all the way home in a blizzard," Kyle exclaimed.

"Mom hates it," Jon added.

"Wait, what? I never said that … How did I suddenly become the bad guy?"

But before I could defend myself any further, they'd left the room. Next, I heard, "Look at that! Wow, what a great tree, guys. You did a fantastic job. I'm really proud of you."

Hello? … what about the new furniture arrangement and all the decorations?

The boys ran back to their TV program and I whispered, "Don't you agree, it's the worst looking tree you've ever seen?"

"It's only a tree," he mumbled and went upstairs for a nap.

ONLY a TREE?

Fortunately, at dinner, the subject didn't come up again. Later that evening, after Bill and the boys went to bed, I turned the lights out and went into the living room. I'd swallowed a boat load of disappointment and felt sour and discouraged inside. *How come nobody in this house gets it—gets me?*

Snow fell heavily outside leaving delicate arching drifts on each window pane. I pulled over a chair, sat down, looked at that tree, picked up my guitar and began to strum. I was not happy with the tree, the men in this house, or myself. *There's nothing wrong with wanting things to look nice, and I'd worked hard on all those ornaments. It would have been really great if someone had paused for one minute to admire what I'd made and maybe pick a favorite.*

I wished I could roll with life, like Bill, without getting so disappointed and irritated. *Lord, where's the all-the-way-through-excellence in me? Why do I have to get so angry when things don't go my way? Maybe Kyle and Jon would have stayed if I hadn't created so much tension. I'm trying to be different."*

Suddenly, a most peculiar thought crossed my mind. *What's the difference between this tree and a tree you would find in a king's palace?*

"Well ... certainly, the shape," I answered.

"The difference between this tree and the tree in a king's palace is that *this* tree never had a *tender*. This one grew up in the fields where the harsh winds and hard winters created its shape. It never had the skilled hands of an arborist who carefully tended to its proper growth."

Tears caught in my throat as I reached for my journal to record what the Lord was saying to me.

"I see you. I see how you serve your family. I see the love behind every decoration you created. This is the spirit of the virtuous women growing in your heart. You are not responsible to shape and ornament your life by yourself. You are in My personal garden. I will tend to you Myself, and I will beautify your life with My fruitfulness."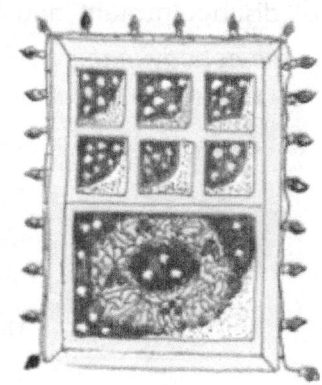

The light emanating from the tree illuminated the entire room. I didn't focus on the uncomely branches anymore. It was the light IN the tree that made it beautiful. Could it be God had the boys pick *this* tree just for this reason? It held the Christmas story, the hope for mankind, born in a homely stable. Then I knew where God wanted my eyes to be—not on the imperfections, but on the hope that He would finish that which He started in me. With one touch from God, our homely, square Christmas tree was transformed into something beautiful … *all because He was in it!*

The next morning, as Bill was leaving for work, he bent down and kissed me tenderly on the lips. "You're awesome," he said softly. "I appreciate all you do."

CHAPTER FOUR

Puttering and Band-aid Decorating

Redecorating my kitchen has been quite a challenge. Our budget at the time didn't allow for anything fancy, so I had to settle for band-aid decorating. One particular evening, I was concentrating on the area around the kitchen sink when I glanced at the clock. It was two in the morning. "What on earth am I doing? I should be in bed!" My kitchen that usually was quite neat, lay in complete disarray. I was *nesting* as Bill calls it. Personally, I call it *puttering*.

The dictionary defines puttering as *engaging in unproductive activities*, meaning *to waste time*. But I'd like to add another definition: puttering around my house can be pure therapy, a productive activity that helps me unwind while attempting to make things attractive. I enjoy moving things for the simple joy of change. I especially love to putter with my plants, shining their leaves, and misting them. However, puttering becomes more like the dictionary's definition when it's generated by discontent, anger, or frustration. I've had enough of those moments in this drafty old farmhouse. When I start banging and slamming things around, it's probably time to evaluate what's going on in my heart.

Any renovation project is a test of patience. There were so many foundational things to repair in this house before the cosmetic improvements I longed for could be made. Sometimes it felt hopeless, kind of like rearranging the deck chairs on the Titanic. My poor husband was not the least bit handy in this area. As a teacher, he could keep a classroom of fourteen-year-olds mesmerized for an entire day, but he had no interest or aptitude for doing drywall or carpentry. Besides, he said he was content with things the way they were when we moved in. (Unlivable) The house belonged to his grandmother, so I guess happy memories helped to cover the imperfections.

I grew up in a new house with wall-to-wall carpeting in the closets. Now I lived in a house with NO closets! I had to stuff things under beds, behind doors, behind the couch, or any other spare space I could find just to get them out of the way. The only extra storage space was a lean-to woodshed that was barely holding on to the end of our house. The basement held no promise either. It was a cobweb-filled dungeon with a hazardous, steep stairway.

My supply of patience rarely met the demand. I longed for walls that were straight, doors that closed, and curtains that didn't blow in the breeze from air streaming through *shut* windows. I hadn't yet grasped the idea that God doesn't make mistakes and that He'd put me in this house for more than a roof over my head. I hadn't yet discovered the stories, and spiritual lessons hidden all around me. So, in the meantime, I suppressed the urge to bulldoze the old place flat. I band-aided my sore attitude with band-aid decorating.

Band-aid Decorating

The wall over the kitchen sink had thick, uneven plaster from a century of repairs. Between paring carrots and doing dishes, I spent hundreds of hours in front of that disreputable old wall. I tried hanging pictures, but they wouldn't lay flat. There were no flat sections! I imagined decorating with everything from a big bay window to a forty-eight-inch TV, but the decree from husband, 'Big Bill,' went out: "The wall is up! *So, leave it alone!*" With the money we had to work with, if something *wasn't* crumbling, it was best not to touch it. There were too many other budget-draining projects that needed immediate attention. I did, however, make my husband promise that as soon as we could afford it, we'd tear down the old plaster and lathes and put up nice ... flat ... even ... drywall.

I visited a country fair one weekend and spotted a handmade pine shelf that seemed like it could be the perfect solution for that wall over the sink—so I bought it. It turned out to be perfect ... *ish*. The giant plaster wart we were trying to conceal made it slightly off balance. (Using a level served no purpose in this house. We did things by *eye*.)

"There you go. Hope that meets your expectations," Bill said, putting his tools away. "That's the best I can do. Good night ... knock yourself out," he said, as he climbed the stairs to bed. He knew this shelf would trigger my putter mania.

He was right. Soon, the kitchen was cluttered with every imaginable knick-knack as I searched for the perfect decorations for my new shelf. A maze of antique tins, 1950s kitchen utensils, baskets, and sprigs of this and that from the field, covered the counters.

I decided to aim for a unique, quaint, early-attic, late-basement look. Anything to make my station at the kitchen sink more interesting. I found a variety of little baskets and perched them alongside an old Punch 'n Judy tin, a little stone lamb, and a floppy, handmade doll from a ministry trip to Missouri. (No dish liquid and scrubbies for this gal!) To camouflage an unsightly crack in the plaster, I hung a neatly folded hand towel on one of the pegs, then stood back to admire my work. "There, she's perfect ... *sort of*. That's the best I can do."

Putter-Procrastination

I must admit there are times when my blithesome-busyness is nothing but procrastination. When I have a job I don't like doing, or a challenging issue to face, the sudden urge to decorate is suspect. For example, the Lord kept nudging me one day to call and apologize to a friend I'd been short with. I hate confrontation and I could feel my flesh resisting. I suddenly felt an urgency to rearrange all the bookshelves in the living room. *I'll call her after I finish this*, I told myself. But hours went by, the school bus came, dinner ensued, and the call was put off. My puttering had become nothing more than plain-old avoidance.

It would have been helpful to know that the virtuous woman was more like the rest of us. Maybe Proverbs 31 could tell us about her frustrations like her price is above rubies, but she regularly throws a fit over the hut she's living in. How about letting us in on some arguments she's had with her husband when it takes him forever to fix the wall over her kitchen sink? (Did they have sinks back then?) On a more personal note, it would be helpful to hear that the Proverbs 31 woman gets bloated and irritable, and pigs out on carbs for at least five days every month.

My dear husband claimed one day that he was having a mid-life crisis. "That's not fair," I complained. "You get to have as many of those as you want. I only get to have ONE!" He responded without missing a beat, "Yeah, but yours lasts for ten years!"

A Poncho and A Problem

Our bathroom had more problems than I could list. First of all, there was only one in the house, and it was *downstairs*. I didn't enjoy going down those steep steps in the middle of the night. The boys got off easy. Bill simply put a blue, enamel pitcher in the upstairs hall ... *Lovely*.

The floor in the bathroom was so slanted, if you sat in the bathtub with three inches of water one cheek would be wet and the other cheek dry!

The walls were crumbling and often we'd find little plaster floaters in the tub. I decided to be helpful one day by tearing down all the plaster and lathes around the tub so Bill only had to drywall. That eliminated the messiest part of the job I knew he hated. To my surprise, he was not happy. I didn't realize how engrained he was in doing one thing at a time. He did not like big projects during the school year. In the meantime, the walls around the bathtub had to be covered with something. So, Bill tacked his army poncho to the studs. "We can use the hood as a pocket to hold the bar soap," he said proudly.

Bill had two weeks of Army duty every summer so the poncho had to be borrowed. It rained heavily one morning as the men stood in formation. Bill soon became the center of attention as bubbles began cascading down his face from the soap residue in his hood.

"Stevens!" barked the commander. "What's the meaning of this? Drop and give me fifty!" This did work for good, however, because Bill came home and immediately hired a company to renovate the bathroom.

The contractor said, "Ma'am, this is the worst bathroom we've ever worked on. You're lucky you didn't end up in the basement sitting on that commode. The floor is completely rotted underneath." *Oh, joy! That's a picture hard to forget.*

Tips From Mary and Martha

Mary and Martha were the sisters of Lazarus, the man Jesus raised from the dead. They were close friends of Jesus and lived in a town called Bethany. Jesus and the disciples were on their way to Jerusalem when they stopped to visit. Martha got distracted by all the preparations for a meal while Mary sat at the feet of Jesus. Martha got a bit perturbed, "Lord, *don't you care* that my sister has left me to do the work by myself? Tell her to help me" (Luke 10:38-42 NIV).

I can't imagine saying, "Don't You care ..." to Jesus, but I know there are times when we're tempted to think that. It stood out to me that Jesus didn't scold Martha for being upset with her sister. Neither did He insist Mary get up and help. I don't believe His tone of voice communicated anger or rebuke. I hear loving instruction, perhaps even a little amusement. "Oh, dear, dear Martha, ...you are worried and upset about many things, but few things are needed—or indeed only one. Mary has chosen what is better, and it will not be taken away from her" (Luke 10:41-42, NIV).

Jesus commended Mary for choosing something that has eternal significance. He didn't tell Martha to stop serving. He did however admonish her about being worried and upset *while* she served.

A Time to Sit and A Time Serve

Discerning when to sit and when to serve will always be a part of the walk of faith. This reminds me of the time my son and his new wife came unexpectedly for a visit. I was thrilled to see them, but at the same time horrified that I had nothing prepared to give them (food is my love language). So, I flew to the kitchen and didn't hear them say they only could stay a few minutes.

"Are you going to join us?" Bill called from the living room.

"C-o-m-i-n-g ..." I sang.

When I finally emerged from the kitchen with a plate full of goodies, they were putting their coats on.

"Are you l-e-a-v-i-n-g?" I asked.

"Sorry, Mom, we told you we only had a little time."

"Ohhh ... I guess I missed that."

My son grabbed a cookie and a chunk of cheese and gave me a kiss on the cheek. Soon they were out the door. I was so disappointed. I kicked myself for fretting over food instead of enjoying their visit. So, I did what any God-fearing, woman of excellence would do—I sat down and polished off the rest of the goodies on the plate (waste-not, want-not).

We all have a little Mary and a little Martha in us. This story certainly highlights the complexity of being a woman. Women are gifted in so many areas and required to wear so many hats. Learning to balance our inner world, while juggling our outer one, requires skill and wisdom. How do we learn this?

The teaching about the virtuous woman in Proverbs 31 comes from a conversation King Lemuel had with his mother. I think it's very interesting that the meaning of the name *Lemuel* points to the secret behind all-the-way-through excellence. It means: *unto God and with God*. Excellence is not the path to Jesus ... being with Jesus is our path to excellence.

That evening I wrote this in my journal:

"It's all about the heart. An intimate relationship with the Lord is not limited to those times when I sit to read His Word and pray. I can keep that same posture of intimacy in my heart no matter what I'm doing. You are with me, Lord, wherever I go. Even puttering can be a time of deep contemplation and prayer. Thank you for my leaky, old farmhouse, Lord. I pray that You will fill it with Your people and Your peace. Excellence will be developed in me when I do everything "unto God and with God" ... even when life limits me to "band-aid" decorating.

CHAPTER FIVE

This Must Be What Trust Feels Like

During our endless renovations, I became a regular visitor at the local hardware store. Often, I'd whisk the kids from the sandbox, load them in the car, and make a mad dash to town. The boys knew the store fairly well, and most of the clerks knew us, so I didn't worry if the boys wandered a bit. But this day...

"Kids, we'll only be here for a few minutes. Stay together and close by so I don't have to hunt for you when it's time to leave." Jon usually stuck to Kyle like glue, no matter what they were doing, but on this day, they lost track of each other.

Kyle and I almost collided as he raced around the corner of the paint aisle. "Mom, where's Jon? I can't find him!"

"I thought you guys were staying together." We hurried toward the front of the store, carefully glancing down every aisle. Jon was nowhere to be seen. The clerk at the front desk said she hadn't seen him, so we asked her to make an announcement over the loudspeaker. I explained that Jon was only four and he might not know what a *checkout* is. So, I asked her to say, "Attention Jon Stevens. Please meet your mommy at the place you pay."

We waited anxiously, and sure enough Jon came running around the corner. He was a sorry sight. His shirt was covered with dirt from the sandbox, and decorated with grape juice. Tears had etched patterns down his sandy cheeks.

"Here you are!" I smiled, trying to keep calm. I bent down on one knee and opened my arms. I could feel his little body trembling. "Jonnie-Babes, you know I would never leave the store without you. If you ever get separated from Mommy or Kyle again, just go to the place where we pay, and I will always find you."

At that moment, Jon's fears felt a whole lot bigger than his trust. He'd never experienced getting separated from Kyle and I at the same time. Being without either of us, in a big store, was just too much.

"I'll never leave you behind," I repeated.

"But *what if* you did?

I could still feel his little body trembling. Kyle patted him on the shoulder, "Sorry, buddy. You're all right."

"Yes, you're all right," I said, taking his hand as we walked to the car.

On the way home, I took the opportunity to talk about the *what-ifs*. "Remember Jonnie-Babes, Jesus is always with you."

"But I can't see Him," he said.

I felt a strange tug in my heart but continued. "I know you

can't see Him, but that's when we have to use our faith. You have to believe He is with you, even when you can't see Him."

Somewhere between rehearsing phone numbers and going over rules about strangers, I looked in the rear-view mirror and both boys were slumped over in a tired, sweaty heap—sound asleep. A few minutes later, I pulled into our driveway and parked the car under the shade of the maple tree beside the porch, rolled down the windows, and let them snooze.

Facing Fear

I sat on the porch for a rest while the boys slept. The sight of my son racing toward me in a panic played over and over in my mind. Tears caught in my throat as I thought of how big and frightening the world must have seemed to him at that moment. *Protect my sons,* I prayed. *Make them invisible to all enemies.* Anxiety knotted my stomach as I thought of all the evil in the world ... all the what-ifs. *You love them even more than I do, Lord. Help me to trust You.* We can't isolate our kids from the world, but we can *insulate* them with a stable home and lots of love and faith.

The story of the disciples out on the sea in a storm came to mind. I opened my Bible to reread the passage. These men were skilled sailors with years of experience, but this storm proved greater than their experience. They also knew Jesus, witnessed Him turn a boy's lunch into a meal for a crowd of more than five thousand, and observed His power as He healed the sick and cast out demons. But they'd never trusted Him in this circumstance before. With the sound of the waves pounding in their ears, their fear totally blinded them.

When I was Jon's age, my father traveled extensively with his job. The longest he was away was two weeks—but to this little four-year-old it seemed like an eternity. Mom always let me know when he was going, but it never quite prepared me for finding him gone. I remember waking up one morning excited to tell him something. I jumped out of bed and ran to his bedroom. He wasn't there. I raced downstairs to the kitchen. He wasn't there either. I clamored down the basement steps to my father's workroom, but he was nowhere to be found.

"Are you looking for Daddy? I told you he's gone on a business trip. Don't worry, he'll be back in a couple of weeks." Mom believed she'd settled things for me, but that didn't fix the hollow feeling in the pit of my tummy. *How long is that? … What if I can't remember what I wanted to tell him? … What if he doesn't come home?*

Just like my son, just like the disciples, and just like all of us, sometimes the magnitude of our circumstances coupled with the fear pounding in our hearts, proves greater than our faith. In my young mind, all I knew was that my dad wasn't there.

A warm August breeze swept across my body bringing a gentle distraction from the intensity of my thoughts. *Help me to trust You completely, Lord."* He reminded me of the scripture I'd read that morning.

"You know when I sit or stand … You chart the path ahead of me … Every moment, you know where I am … You are thinking about me constantly!"
(From Psalm 139, The Living Bible).

I was still lost in my thoughts when Jon's sleepy little face suddenly appeared in the open car window. "Mommm...?" His hair, all sweaty and matted, stuck against his temples. Even at a distance, I could still see dried tear streaks on his face. I smiled and sent him a little wave. Then, he disappeared back down beside his brother to sleep a little longer.

I decided to go inside and start dinner. The boys could not see me through the dark doorway to the kitchen, but I could see them—and I was watching.

You see me ... You chart my path ... Your thoughts toward me are constant ..." I picked up my paring knife and began to prepare a salad for dinner—I didn't even mind that I was paring carrots again. The words of the Psalmist played over and over in my thoughts like a joy-filled, healing balm. "Hmmm," I contemplated. "This must be what trust feels like!

CHAPTER SIX

Mom of the Block

There seemed to be a constant parade of kids flowing through our house during the summer months. Nearly a dozen little bodies crossed our threshold one particular day to get a drink or use the bathroom. None of them had been invited. My efforts to plan my day never worked in the summer. I *tried* to keep up with my housework, but that usually went out the window. If I did clean, it wouldn't stay that way for very long, so, why bother?

Usually the boys played outside all day. We had a huge cast iron kettle in the yard intended for geraniums, but the boys turned it into a mud hole. All the kids in the neighborhood wanted to come here to play. Thanks to grandparents and a few garage sales we had enough Tonka trucks for everybody.

There was also a constant flow of children to my door to get a drink. I stopped one little guy making his third visit for a drink. "Hey, buddy, don't you have running water at your house?" He stared up at me blankly and said, "But, I thursee *here*."

Drinking all that water resulted in a steady stream of traffic to our facilities. My husband and I were trying to squeeze as many years as possible out of our tiny septic tank, so all those flushes concerned us. I considered posting a sign on the door: *No Bathroom Privileges Except for Paying Customers*, but only a few kids could read! Thankfully, they weren't watering my bushes.

The year we finally sprang for a new septic tank, everyone assembled in the yard to watch. This kind of renovation is no fun— because who's going to admire your investment? Bill and I stood around the giant hole, silently blotting our tears, as three years' worth of vacation money got lowered into the ground. The kids in the neighborhood loved the project because the backhoe left a lot of fresh dirt to play in. *Oh, joy.* (Maybe a pay toilet would have been a good idea.)

The next problem *trickling* away our money came from the constant need to replace the hinges on the bathroom door. You see, the lower hinge was at the exact height of the commode. With all those little boys, a serious rust problem developed. The top hinge remained bright and shiny, but the rusty hinge at the bottom proved no one could aim. I told them a hinge is NOT a target, but that didn't work. Eventually, we hired a carpenter to turn the door around so it opened on the other side. We figured we'd earn back that investment by not having to buy so many hinges. Bill called it: "*trickle*-down economics."

As a sincere wanna-be orange-all-the-way-through woman of excellence, I prayed that God would give me a divine infusion of grace for patience. I wanted to be a positive Christian example for all these thirsty "pee-ons." However, that level of spiritual proficiency had not yet reached my feet. The truth remains that it's not what we *say,* as much as what we *do,* that makes the lasting impression.

I'm sure the kids in the neighborhood will remember the day I wasn't like a carrot for God. They were happily playing in the dirt when I caught a glimpse of the neighbor's dog digging up my annuals for the third time. I bolted into the yard screaming at the top of my lungs, whipping a waffle iron cord over my head. The kids hit the dirt! They didn't know I was screaming at a dog. They watched wide-eyed as I went shrieking into the next yard.

"I know I scared them," I told Bill later. "They hit the dirt like there was some sort of incoming missile. I tried to recover my image with some cookies. Poor kids will probably grow up wondering why they crave sugar every time they see a dog."

"Or duck every time they see a Christian?" Bill added dryly.

I had so much growing to do. My patience hardly ever

matched the demand. Discouragement left footprints across my heart every time I blew it. I started each day determined to do better, but somehow between the dog's antics, and all the neighbors sending their kids to play at my house, I'd lose it.

It wasn't only what happened around here that wore me thin; it lay in my unrealistic expectations. They were too impractical. God never promised to make me all-the-way-through *perfect*. He promised to make me a woman of *excellence*.

Perfectionism is a brutal taskmaster that regards anything short of perfection as unacceptable and looks at failure as personal worthlessness. Perfectionism robs us of spontaneity and trust because it's motivated by fear and the need to be in control.

I'll never forget the conversation my husband and I had on the way home from the hospital after Kyle, our first son, was born. Tears grabbed at my throat as I looked down into his sweet little face. "What if he doesn't like me?" I cried.

Bill reached across the seat and patted my shoulder, "I wouldn't worry about it. It's inevitable."

"No, I'm serious. It's not funny. Even the experts don't agree on how to raise a child." I sniffled. "I'll never get it right."

Bill thought for a minute. "First of all, you're too hard on yourself. This is how I see it. We won't get it perfect, that's for sure, but we'll love him with all our might. We'll pray often, apologize freely, and do the best we can."

As it turned out, Kyle was an easy baby. He slept through the night after the first week and almost never spit up. I thought I'd conquered motherhood until Jon came along. Jon didn't sleep through the night until he was two years old. He watched his big brother do things … like walk. Jon had barely begun to crawl, but he wanted to walk. So, whenever Kyle scurried past him, Jon would scream at the top of his lungs. Once he started walking peace was reestablished. Then, he observed Kyle could talk in sentences ... *s-c-r-e-a-m* ... he could raise the roof! Goodbye, quiet house.

My sweet husband could see that chasing two rambunctious boys all day was wearing me out. He offered to watch them on a regular basis so I could recharge in the hammock. *Oh bliss*!

All the boys in our neighborhood were at least two years older than Jon. He'd get so frustrated trying to keep up with the "big guys," he'd explode. I taught him to pray when he started getting angry. "If you have trouble praying by yourself, come right home and we'll pray together." He took it to heart. One afternoon as I was having tea with a group of ladies, the kitchen door flew open, and in ran my red-faced son. "MOOOMMM ... Q-U-I-C-K ... WE GOTTA P-R-A-Y! ... I'M GONNA ESSPODE!

A Gift of Love

There was nothing I wanted more than to be a good mom, but it seemed all the other moms I knew were doing a better job. There were some good parenting books available, but frankly I didn't want to find out how badly I was doing. So, I tried to follow my husband's advice: pray often, apologize freely, and do my best.

I returned home from a ministry trip late one night and discovered a half dozen boys sound asleep on the living room floor. Obviously, my guys had convinced their father to let them have a sleep-over.

These kids could test the best of moms, but now they lay nestled in their blankets all pink-cheeked and peaceful. Some still wore traces of peanut butter and jelly, a little smear of chocolate, and a crusty mustache of milk. I smiled. Every one of them had enriched my life and I felt grateful they liked being at our house.

The rich tones of the antique clock in the living room blended with their soft, slumbering sounds. An overwhelming sense of love enveloped my heart - a love beyond myself. For a brief moment, God was letting me experience His love for them.

I noticed a strange lump in the center of the dining room table under a bath towel. Hesitating, I braced myself for any one of a million possibilities and slowly lifted the towel.

It turned out to be a rough-cut, circular piece of wood about ten inches across and about an inch thick. A handmade Kleenex carnation glued at the top embellished a glittering sequined message carefully glued in bold letters: *MOM OF THE BLOCK*.

I stood motionless, reading it over and over. "Lord, how can this be? I can't believe they made this for me." Gracing the bottom of the plaque were all their names.

Out from under a quilt popped a curly-headed visitor. He staggered unsteadily past me in the dark, making his way to the bathroom. Since the light switch was too high for him to reach, I decided to help him. He didn't seem interested in the light. In fact, he wasn't even awake. Out of sheer habit, he scooted behind the door and sprayed where the old hinge *used* to be, leaving a nice little puddle for me on the floor.

I tucked him back under his blanket and whispered, "Got running water at your house yet?"

Jon rolled over and said, "Hi, Mom. I asked some kids to spend the night. Is it okay?"

I chuckled, "It's okay, Jonnie Babes, go back to sleep." I put my plaque where everyone was sure to see it, and whispered, "Jon, I love my surprise ..."

As I headed upstairs for bed, I heard, "Hey Mom, can you make pancakes for us in the morning?"

CHAPTER SEVEN

The Coon Dog Saga – Part One

Kids are greatly influenced by the labels we put on them, but what about animals? Do they count? I read somewhere that people unconsciously choose the canine version of themselves. Considering the kind of dog we picked, this idea was especially repugnant to me.

In a moment of soft-hearted insanity, we bought this floppy-eared coon dog as a surprise for our son, Kyle. We knew nothing of this breed, except they were great hunters. Perhaps we should have questioned why the man selling these dogs wanted us to pick her up at midnight, and turn our headlights off when we pulled into his driveway. The man also never looked us in the eyes. Perhaps we should have been alerted by the whirlwind transaction he sailed us through before jumping in his truck and leaving town (A bit of an exaggeration, I admit). The boys called her Babe, but later, I'm embarrassed to admit, she was labeled "you-big-fat-dumb-thing," by guess who?

My husband and I bought the dog believing this was the perfect opportunity to teach our son responsibility. Little did we know that Babe (pronounced Babe-ith by Jon) would challenge the best of dog trainers, let alone us. The first challenge arrived almost immediately. Babe did not accept our house. She refused to settle, running frantically from window to window trying to escape.

The next day when the UPS man greeted our new dog, he quickly informed us that coon dogs preferred to live outside "on a strong chain or fenced in with a high fence." *Hmmm, why did he say that?* That statement turned out to be a prophetic warning, because Babe-ith soon became his arch-enemy.

On his advice, we purchased a large dog house and placed it on a small hill where she could see everything. We bought her a bed, a long chain guaranteed not to choke her, a dish, and a rawhide bone—all the right stuff to ensure Babe's happiness.

My vision of a sleeping hound lounging by the wood stove proved seriously flawed. Any time we tried to bring Babe inside, she'd frantically race from window to window smearing the glass with her nose. Or, she'd just stand in the middle of the room staring sullenly into space. We were confused.

Serious reservations about this mutt began to plague me. She was unlike any dog we'd ever had. I found myself muttering negatives under my breath every time I passed her. "Why don't you go lie down, you big fat dumb thing?" I'd growl.

Alone on her hill, Babe would stand and bark. She wasn't barking at something or barking to come in. She wasn't lonesome for our company. She could care less about people. Babe wasn't interested in responding to her name, or having her ears scratched. She just wanted to bark—morning, noon, and night.

The Dreaded Swamp

As the days dragged on, another problem surfaced. Across the road from our house are five acres of swamp land, home to countless raccoons. We noticed Babe showing signs of alertness we had not seen before. Now, she not only lived to bark, eat and ignore people, she lived to hunt raccoons. Toss-the-stick games were meaningless to one who knew her calling. Babe was destined to go where no other 95-pound, mentally challenged, coon dog had ever gone before. She was on her way to climbing trees, diving into freezing cold swollen streams, brawling with a half-crazed fifty-pound beaver, and getting hopelessly wedged inside old logs. To be sure, this coon dog had a future.

Babe's hankering to hunt grew as she matured. Her once, semi-cute yips became thunderous, primal howls as each tantalizing aroma drifted up from the fields. We even got hang-up phone calls from the neighbors when she'd break her chain and escape to the swamp. We had to get this dog in the house—or move!

The tension between Babe and I continued to mount. My little mutterings became bold-faced pronouncements. "You big-fat-dumb-thing. You are an embarrassment to the entire dog world. You challenge the accepted truth that God never makes mistakes."

Babe let us know, in no uncertain terms, that she was an un-moldable beast. She was fast earning the title, "Coon Dog from hell." It never dawned on me to pray.

Desperation settled in. It was the dog or me. In spite of all my mother's training to BE NICE, this dog managed to bring out the 'beast' in me. Radical transformation offered the only hope.

I finally concluded this was a job for Jesus. The minute I turned heavenward, conviction came. To be honest, I'd hoped for a little sympathy for having to spend my days with this *thing* of a dog. Instead, came the kind of conviction that takes your breath away. God showed me the ugliness of the labels I'd put on Babe, and how she was heartily living up to my negative expectations.

The Ultimate Humiliation

God's remedy shocked me: *"Repent and ask the dog to forgive you,"* He said.
You've got to be kidding me. "Lord, am I hearing You correctly? This is a dog we're talking about here." The conviction in my spirit let me know He was serious. I knew I had to obey.

Hesitantly, I slipped outside. There she sat in front of her half-chewed-up dog house, in the center of a freshly dug hole in the dirt. I glanced around the neighborhood to assure myself no one could see me. Then I knelt down in the dirt. I've heard of repenting in dust and ashes, but this? Without warning, the strangest thing happened. Babe looked me in the eyes for the *first time*. We connected. Could it be, the beast actually possessed *feelings?*

Taking her dirty face in my hands, I swallowed hard and said,

"Forgive me, Babe. You're not a big-fat-dumb-thing; you're not a dog from hell."

Miraculously, I felt a sudden surge of emotion and actually got a little tearful. One by one I peeled off the labels I'd branded her with until no more negative thoughts came to mind. Then, I gave her a big hug. This dog *never* let me hold her before. She sat there as if she understood. After a nice conversation (one-sided of course), I went back to my chores with peace in my heart that I'd done what the Lord asked.

Later that evening, we went to visit Bill's mom. She proudly presented me with a hand-crocheted afghan she'd just finished.

"Oh, Bernice, this is gorgeous," I exclaimed. "Thank you. I love it."

"It's for Babe," she said.

"Huh?"

Bill came to my rescue. "Nice, Mom, I'm sure Babe will get a lot of … uh … use out of it."

"Marjorie, you have to keep that sweet baby warm in that old farmhouse."

Oh, Lord, help me here… Sweet Baby? I bristled inside. *Isn't that taking positive reinforcement a little far, Lord?*

When we returned home, even Bill noticed a difference in Babe. I hadn't told him about our conversation earlier that day. "What's up with Babe?" he said. "She's happy to see us. Maybe she's sick?"

We unhooked her from the chain and instead of charging straight for the swamp, she trotted to the front door to come inside. "Look at her! She wants to come inside," exclaimed Kyle. I tried to minimize the notion that *my* change of heart made that much difference, but it was unmistakable.

Then it happened—she *walked* into the house, without running from window to window, and *sat* down. Astonished, the family stood staring at her. For the first time, Babe was not only *inside*, she was inside and *happy*.

I unwrapped her surprise, "Look what we have for you, girl. A hand-crocheted blanket." She eyed it expressionlessly and didn't move.

"Maybe she doesn't know what to do with it" the kids ventured. "Show her, Mom."

"I'm not getting down on the floor. Let's try this..." I held up one end of the blanket, let the other end drag across the floor and coaxed Babe to come lie down. After staring blankly into space for several minutes, she slowly walked onto the blanket circled three times and flopped down with a sigh. I completely covered her head with the rest of the blanket. Babe didn't move. It was as if she'd been waiting for this moment since she came to live with us.

"A dog TART!" Jonathan exclaimed.

"Indeed," Bill laughed. "Leave it to my mom—food and warmth."

Her blanket heaved slightly and Babe fell sound asleep. Content at last, with only one minor adjustment to our long-awaited expectation: instead of being a dog-ON-a-rug, Babe wanted to be a dog-IN-a-blanket.

My journal entry that day read:

"It's not only our words that influence others. We cannot mask a bitter spirit even with pleasantries. Our attitudes are communicated when words are not expressed. Words of acceptance are nice to hear, but even dogs can tell you, there's nothing like acceptance from the heart to make you understand you are home.

CHAPTER EIGHT

The Coon Dog Saga – Part Two

Now Babe reigned. The living room was her throne room, the crocheted blanket her cape. In fact, she became a permanent lump in the center of our house. It was nearly impossible to get her to move. That was annoying enough, but you haven't lived until you've been awakened in the middle of a cold winter's night with Babe staring you in the face. I knew that look all too well: *Wake up, I'm cold … you have to cover me!*

Once again, I'm embarrassed to say, Babe turned out to be an effective catalyst in my evolution to all-the-way-through-excellence, but not without challenging the progress on a daily basis. Other dogs appreciate snuggling and pleasant walks on a spring day. Not Babe. She lived for the moment the refrigerator door opened and she could get a strong whiff of its contents. It was like watching the manifestation of a dog demon. Babe's eyes rolled back in her head, her nostrils flared, and a steady stream of drool pooled on the floor.

Peering through the holes of her crocheted blanket, she often sat near the refrigerator—hoping … if that didn't produce results, she'd get up, her blanket still draped over her head, and move methodically through the house looking for the tiniest morsel of food. When "vacuuming" the floor offered no more reward, she'd flop down wherever she was and resume her dog-tart status. "Babe, your inability to control your appetite is really troubling!"

Babe's roundness didn't trouble her—she was secure with her hefty 'tarted' life. Heaven for her was anything left unguarded on the kitchen counters. She could inhale an entire loaf of bread in the time it took me to butter a single slice. All she'd leave behind is a slimy plastic bread wrapper licked into the corner of the kitchen.

I'll never forget the day I was preparing meatballs for my son's graduation party. I had a giant metal bowl filled with about ten pounds of ground venison, bread crumbs, garlic, Worcestershire sauce, raw eggs, and onion. I left the bowl of meat on the counter to briefly step out of the room. When I returned, the bowl was still on the counter but it was nearly licked clean! I shrieked in horror, while Babe sat on her blanket belching shamelessly.

Babe's food compulsion soon shifted to a new low. She found her way into the pantry one day. Discovering the cabinet door open, she gobbled down an entire bag of marshmallows, two pounds of jelly beans, and a bag of potato chips. After that, Babe took to spending her days sitting in the pantry—waiting. She learned that when the front door slammed, the vibration would cause the pantry cupboard door to creak open, and her gluttonous-gobbling would begin.

I've heard that children will mirror the behavior of their parents, but I wonder … does that theory also apply to dogs? I was afraid to find out.

No one else in the family was disturbed by Babe's uncontrollable appetite, but it really bothered me. It seems she only emerged from her blanket long enough to peruse the waste paper baskets and sniff for crumbs. She'd go for anything: Hall's Eucalyptus wrappers, Kleenex, old gum … you name it. We spent outrageous amounts of money buying diet dog food, but it wasn't what Babe ate *at* meals that was the problem, it was all the garbage she ate *in between* meals. Raccoon hunting brought only a temporary slenderizing to her ever-broadening beam. All that time in her *dog-tart* was having its obvious effects.

"Bill, I think Babe has a food compulsion. I'm going to look for a twelve-step program for fat dogs."

Bill chuckled, "Heck, if it's compulsion we're talking about, why not go for twenty-four steps?"

On one rare occasion, I bought some Oreo cookies for the boys. Soon, only *three* cookies remained. The challenge: two boys and three cookies. They did what boys do, they wrestled for it *on the couch* while Babe watched. As soon as I heard their ruckus, I rushed downstairs. When the boys heard me coming, they hid the last cookie down the side of my *new*, plaid loveseat. I sent the boys outside and then returned upstairs. Babe watched the whole thing. When I disappeared, the dog got up, dragged her blanket over to the couch, stuck her head down the side of the cushion, found the lone Oreo cookie, and proceeded to dig for more.

"THAT DOG SHOULD BE *STRANGLED*!" I wailed as I picked up shredded foam rubber and ripped upholstery fabric from the living room floor. "God, You *have* to do *something* about this dog. She's out of control ..."

The Truth Hurts

I stewed about my couch for days. I was at my wit's end. Every time I prayed for God's intervention with the dog it seemed He pointed back to me.

I searched through my journals one day for a particular entry, but couldn't find it. It occurred to me a table of contents would be helpful. I reviewed a couple of diaries each day making notes of the important parts on the front page. What I discovered in the process startled me. Instead of writing something like: "Kyle got an "A," or "Jon played drums at a talent show," I had page after page listing the foods I'd eaten that day. Agonizing prayers followed every failed attempt to measure up to my strict eating regimens. *Lord, help me lose weight. Please command a breakthrough for me.*

I didn't leave my concerns with Him. Instead, I tried harder, condemning myself for every imperfection. My journal entries were filled with depression and discouragement, revealing my lack of faith in that area of my life. I also could see I had no appreciation for the body and good health God had given me. *Lord, I have a problem ... I'm the one with the eating disorder.*

If I ate right, I'd record: "*I was good* today." If I ate unhealthily, I'd write, "*I was bad.*" No matter how hard I tried, or how sorry I was, there was little change in my behavior. It seemed I had no ability to resist sugar. To the contrary, I craved it. Whenever I ate wrong, I'd become afraid … *I'm going to get fat. I'm going to get diabetes.* I needed God to deliver me. I didn't understand that I was dealing with something even greater than the threat of weight gain and diabetes.

All the aunts on my father's side were extremely overweight. Mom didn't want me to follow in their footsteps, so every time I reached for a cookie, she'd remark, "You don't want to get fat like Aunt Peg, DO YOU?" If Mom saw an obese woman in the store she'd mutter, "I don't know HOW she can ALLOW herself to get like THAT."

I wasn't born with a slender figure like my mom. I was built with the same frame as my father's side of the family— big-boned, broad-shouldered, and *square*. Dad said I walked like Sam Huff, a linebacker for the New York Giants. He made me practice walking with a book on my head.

Eating and shame grew side-by-side in my mind. Guilt says, "I *did* something bad." Shame says, "I *AM* bad."

The further I read in my journals the more shocked I became to see how I'd been measuring my *self-worth* in calories and pant sizes. I'd tried every conceivable diet over the years, all of them short-lived. The most startling part is the self-loathing that followed every crumb I consumed. I had no tolerance for the slightest slip. I had no grace for myself, no acceptance, and little faith that God would help me. I wanted Him to change me so that I could finally be happy with myself. He wanted me to first accept myself the way He made me.

God's word says that we are fearfully and *wonderfully made* (Psalm 139:14). The phrase is translated from the Hebrew word *pala*, which reinforces our individual craftsmanship and purpose. This phrase means we are created "distinct", "set apart," or "distinguished" from other creations.[4] Often our significance is clouded by what we've been taught, by forces of evil, our own sinful nature, or the sinful acts of others. But the truth is we are uniquely designed *by* God, and made in His image.

I closed my eyes and thought about what I'd been saying about myself. *Forgive me, Lord. "I am fearfully and wonderfully made."* God gave me this body for a purpose and I need to begin this journey by being grateful.

There's a mysterious awesomeness about the way He shapes each one of us. We're crafted with reverent holiness and love. For us to condemn the body God *created* grieves His heart, and we remain *caught*.

A Woman Accused

I was puzzled when my thoughts drifted to the story of the woman caught in the act of adultery. A crowd gathered to hear Jesus teach when the sound of a boisterous scuffle was heard at

---

[4] What Does Psalm 139 mean by 'Fearfully and Wonderfully Made'? Lori Stanley Roeleveld, contributing editor
https://www.christianity.com/wiki/bible/what-does-psalm-139-mean-fearfully-and-wonderfully-made.html

the door of the Temple. Teachers of the law and Pharisees barged into the courtyard dragging a woman behind them. I could almost smell the pungent odor of their dusty, sweaty robes in the sweltering heat of the day. Their condemning voices echoed off the stone walls. I identified with how that woman must have felt being thrown into the center of angry accusers.

I imagined myself standing in that courtyard watching the events unfold, when suddenly I became the one slouched in the center of the accusing mob. I was the one being pummeled by angry, hate-filled accusations. *You're bad ... you've broken the laws of health and deserve to be punished!* Every word came wrapped in shame cordoning off all hope of deliverance. I didn't dare look up, but a strange force lifted my head. To my surprise, all the accusers had vanished, and only one loving face remained.

"Where are your accusers, daughter?" He whispered.

His words washed over me and tears coursed down my cheeks. How had I allowed this to happen? My accusers were all in my mind. *I* was the voice of condemnation!

The sound of the school bus interrupted my concentration. The boys clamored through the front door tossing their bookbags on the floor. "I'm FIRST..." Jon yelled, racing toward the bathroom.

"Boys, no fighting," I called. My thoughts were far away as I placed a hearty dollop of peanut butter in a bowl with cut-up apples. We sat down at the kitchen table and the boys told me about their day. I glanced over at Babe peacefully basking in the center of a shaft of sunlight streaming through the living room window. Her blanket rose and fell blissfully. *That difficult dog has done it again... put me in the* classroom *with the Lord.*

CHAPTER NINE

The Coon Dog Saga – Part Three

The next morning, as soon as the boys left for school, I got my journal and Bible and settled in my favorite chair by the window. *Lord, please help me see what You are trying to show me.* I returned to the story of the woman caught in the act of adultery.

Often when I read scripture one word will jump out at me. Previously, it had been about her *accusers*. This time the word

"caught" leaped off the page. That piqued my curiosity so I looked up the Greek definition. First, *caught* means *to lay hold of, or seize.*[5] The woman had been laid hold of, and seized, in the act of sinning. I couldn't relate to that part of the definition. But *caught* also carries the sense of being *ensnared* or *entangled* by something. That's how I felt about my obsession with weight and diets. I wanted permanent lifestyle changes so I wouldn't have to think about it anymore. But, instead, I kept sliding into old habits. I wanted to be free from the yo-yo world that kept me discouraged and condemning myself. Clearly, I was *ensnared* by something. Something in my thinking had me tangled up and *stuck*.

Jesus spoke to the woman's accusers, "Let any one of you who is without sin be the first to throw a stone at her." Then He stooped down a second time and wrote something on the ground. Whatever He wrote brought strong conviction on the accusers and one by one they left until there were none.

"Woman, where are they? Has no one condemned you?" Jesus continued, "Then neither do I condemn you. Go and leave your life of sin" (John 8:11).

When I read "Leave your life of sin," I felt frustrated. I'd been trying to "leave" this problem for years. I knew He led me to this Scripture, but there was definitely something I wasn't getting. The

---

[5] Strong's Concordance. https://biblehub.com/greek/2638.htm

woman could avoid those unholy relationships, but how do I go and *eat* no more?

Little did I know, the Lord was planning to use Babe again to teach me. That evening, somehow Babe got off her chain and made a mad dash for the swamp. Bill whistled, Kyle called, and I prayed, but no Babe. The swamp is no place for humans when it's dark, so we had no choice but to wait.

Across that jungle of weeds and muck Babe's premortal howls echoed across the valley bringing on the usual flurry of hang-up phone calls. The neighbors were just as frustrated with that dog as we were.

"God, p-l-e-a-s-e get that dog home!" I pleaded. Sure enough, about an hour later Babe staggered in. I wanted to lambaste her, but noticed her eyes were nearly swollen shut. I looked closer and discovered dozens of marble-sized lumps covering her snout … her ears … down the front of her chest!

"OH, NO! BILL, Babe has some kind of weird swamp disease!" (It was startling how much I suddenly cared) "We have to take her to emergency!"

We'd been to the emergency before. The month before she consumed an entire box of rat poison and we had to have her stomach pumped. That visit cost us $175. I tried to make a swap with the vet, the bill for the dog, but he didn't want her either. Now this!

We rolled her lumpy self into the car and drove to the vet emergency. The doctor took one look at her and laughed, "Oh my, where has she been?"

"The swamp—barking like a fool."

"That must have been some raccoon," he chuckled. "How long was she there?"

"I don't want to talk about it," I groaned. "Ask the neighbors. They can tell you."

"I see," he snickered. "She was so fixated on that raccoon that she didn't realize she was being attacked by mosquitoes!"

"You're kidding me! *Mosquitoes*?"

"Yup ... hundreds of them ... maybe thousands." His grin never left his face as he made notes in Babe's file.

"I hope you're including *mentally challenged* ... or ... *dumb-as-a-door-dog* in your records? Why didn't she realize she was being eaten alive and have the sense to move?"

The vet shrugged, "She's a DOG! That's what dogs do. Take her home and let her be."

"I'll let her be..." I grumbled as I wrote a check.

On the way home, Babe resumed her favorite position on the passenger side of the front seat. Unlike a typical dog, who bends forward or out the window, Babe leans back against the seat like a human being. I reached in the backseat and got her baseball cap and sat it on her head. The look on the guy's face in the car next to us when we stopped at a traffic light almost made the whole event worth it.

We needed to have a little heart-to-heart. "Now look, Babe, you and I have been through a lot together and I think I've earned the right to speak into your life. You should have stopped barking up that tree—you were being eaten alive."

I realized I'd said something a whole lot smarter than my

reasoning abilities. By the time I tucked Babe in her blanket and covered her head, the sun was coming up. I got a cup of coffee and went to the couch to read my Bible.

I kept thinking about my words: *barking up that tree is eating you alive.* I've been focused on this problem for so long it was consuming me. I randomly opened the Scriptures to Jonah 2:8 (NKJV) and read, "Those who regard worthless idols forsake their own mercy." A footnote included: *or, they forfeit the grace available to them.* I gasped and read it again. *Is this me? Am I forfeiting the grace I need to change?* It never occurred to me that my problem could be connected to idolatry.

It's easy to see that our culture is *full* of idols. Women's sense of worth is too often tied to appearance or to the ability to achieve some level of perfection. Photoshopped models dot every publication touting the shallow values of rich, thin, and beautiful. Measuring ourselves against these images too often leads to self-loathing and discouragement.

My thoughts went back to the woman "caught" and I wondered how many women are snared in the net of harmful behaviors because they measure themselves against these manufactured, unattainable ideals?

"But Lord, I don't understand how You say 'go and sin no more' and not explain *how to do that*? I'd love to find the switch to turn this problem off once and for all, so I'll never be tempted to eat junk again."

I sensed the Holy Spirit telling me to go back to the story and read the next verse for the key. Jesus said, "I am the light of the world. He who follows Me will never walk in darkness, but will have the light of life.

He who follows Me...

"He who follows Me..." leaped off the page. To me, that implies turning away from the direction you *had been* going and go in a completely *new* direction. Just as the woman caught in the act of adultery had to learn to develop healthy relationships that didn't break God's laws, I had to learn to develop new patterns of eating that didn't break the rules of health I was learning.

I grew up eating Twinkies, Jell-O, hotdogs and drinking Kool-Aid. Mom used to buy Millbrook white bread. I remember my brother and me condensing a whole slice into a ½ inch cubes so we could fling them at each other like spit-balls. My tastebuds were conditioned to want those empty calories that are not only unhealthy, they're addictive. God wanted to lead me into a wholesome, healthier lifestyle. That would require depending on the Holy Spirit to teach me, and empower me to apply what I learned.

I hear over and over that diets don't work because they're short-lived. I proved that theory true. It's all about lifestyle changes. I heard Jesus saying He will lead me in a completely *new* direction. No more white-knuckled self-discipline. No more measuring myself against false standards. No more barking up trees ... follow His lead.

I felt a wonderful freedom enter my soul as I picked up my journal. "Father, help me to lay it all down ... I renounce this idol, in Jesus' name, and embrace the grace You have given through Your Son, Jesus Christ. Cause me to desire healthy things. Change my tastebuds. Thank you, Lord for the promise in Philippians 1:6, that You will complete the work You have started in me."

I looked down at Babe snoring peacefully near my feet. "Sweet baby..." I reached down and patted her head. "We're okay, girl ... you and me ... we're okay."

My journal entry that day read:

> "Learning to walk in the Spirit, especially in the area of healthy mind and body habits, is a life-long journey. New patterns of behavior don't happen overnight. It takes time and dependency on the Holy Spirit. There's no room in my life for self-loathing or condemnation. When I stumble, I need to confess it quickly, and get back on the right path. Lord, help me to recognize the lies. They don't have any place in my thinking. Help me to hold on to the truth that I am *fearfully* and *wonderfully* made."

Father, forgive me. I renounce the lie that says my value is dependent upon my appearance or my performance. Forgive me for looking to food as a source of comfort, and my appearance as a source of confidence. Forgive me for hating my body, or comparing myself to others. Thank you for the blood of my Lord Jesus Christ, that cleanses me from sin. Help me to glorify You in my body as well as my thoughts. I trust You to help me make healthy lifestyle choices. Fill me with Your Holy Spirit and help me follow You. In Jesus name, Amen.

CHAPTER TEN

The Dreaded Cheese Curl

We all have our secrets. There's nothing better than the feeling of getting things out in the open with someone who is safe and trustworthy. I've found that struggles become less overwhelming when shared with a friend.

With that in mind, I'm going to be completely transparent with you. I am a recovering cheese curl junkie. For me, there's no way to eat them in moderation. The first crunch sets me off.

I'm amazed at how easy it is to lie to oneself. I'll lay down a new course to all-the-way-through healthy eating, then tell myself: "A few won't hurt," or "It's a special occasion." Or, if I purchase said temptation telling myself, "It's for the kids." Which too often disappears before they get any.

"Mommm, got any 'nacks?" asks Jonathan.

"Hmmm ... Sorry, honey, I thought I had some. Your father probably ate them." (Yeah, right.)

I gob-ba bulb-uh on my lib-peb!

I used to eat Nachos every night. I must have developed an allergy to those nasty snacks, because as I ate them, I could feel a bulbous canker sore rising on my lip.

Any kind of greasy-crunchy-starchy-carbos is a siren call when I'm bored, lonesome, or overtired. I never crave broccoli when I feel blue, do you?

With the sultry call of the cheese curl, not even the threat of ingesting chemicals was a deterrent. I'd met my nemesis. Once the taste of salt and cheddar were on my tongue, I was a goner. Oh, the crunch. Oh, the artificial cheese aftertaste. Oh, the orange dust left to lick off my fingers after the last curl disappeared. It's not a snack, it's an experience.

Then there's the art of eating cheese curls. You can woof them down by the fist-full like some people I know, or delicately consume them with style and thoughtful enjoyment. I eventually worked up to 30 delicate nibbles per curl. (Even though my mother taught me not to play with my food). This pastime is similar to seeing how long you can suck on a lifesaver before it breaks in two.

In the depths of my cheese curl addition, my cuticles often carried a hint of orange, and my back teeth had the lingering remains of cheddar paste. If I sat down to relax and read a book, things didn't feel right without nibbling on the curvy crisp. I savored each moment with my flaky friend. But every indulgence left me with soul-wrenching condemnation. I knew they were adding girth to my ever-broadening hips, besides being unhealthy.

Cheese curl crumbs adhered to my flannel pajamas and left a residue on the sheets one night. "Honey, what's that orange stuff on the sheets?"

"Oh, that … I bought some orange-colored body powder." *Oh, the shame. Now I've added lying to my fleshly sin.*

"I didn't know they made powder that smells like cheese!"

Here was my opportunity to come clean … but I silenced that thought with the excuse that Bill had to get to work. *I'll tell him later,* I told myself.

For a long time, my husband unwittingly supported my habit. If I was sad, sick, whiny, grouchy or bored, he knew just what would cheer me up. He'd surprise me with a bag from the 7-Eleven. Sweet guy.

I was *trying* to quit. I'd crushed many half-eaten bags of cheese curls under my feet. I've run them under water, thrown them out the car window, locked them in the trunk of my husband's car and made him promise not to give me the keys no matter how I threatened him. I made declarations, turned over multiple leaves, even banned them from the house, but sooner or later I'd cave in.

I never told anyone, not even my best friend. I carried the burden and condemnation by myself. I had shelves full of books on nutrition, but what I needed was not more *information*. I needed *impartation*. If God didn't give me the power to overcome, I knew the dreaded cheese curl would be my undoing for the rest of my life.

One day, in an attempt to stop myself from consuming an entire bag, I attempted to flush them down the toilet. To my horror, I discovered *cheese curls don't flush . . . they float!* As I waited for the water in the tank to fill so I could flush again, I heard my husband come through the front door. *Oh no! What was I to do?* I gave it one more frantic flush and down they went. *Thank you, God.*

I emerged from the bathroom as if nothing was wrong. "Hi honey, how was your day?"

"Long," he said, passing me to use the facilities.

Phew, that was close. But as soon as he flushed the toilet I heard, **"WHAT THE ...? MARJ ... Have you been eating cheese curls again?"**

I needed to come clean. But, could I tell the man who already had a long day? "Oh, by the way, I am a cheese curl addict?" No.

"Uh, don't you remember, we had the septic tank emptied? I think he must have put in a new kind of absorbent in the tank that happens to look like cheese curls . . .?"

"Yeah . . . right."

Bill knew the truth. I thought I was hiding it from him, but he could see what I was doing to myself. Pride, and the love of my sin, kept me from admitting the truth. I needed to surrender. I had to desire wholeness more than the taste of cheese. Later that night, I opened my Bible.

"For nothing is secret that will not be revealed, nor anything hidden that will not be known and come to light." (Luke 8:17)

My secret was not a secret to God. He saw me nibbling at night. He saw the cheese curl bag hidden in the backseat of my car. He saw my hiding places. He saw me guarding my stash from the kids. He heard the cover-ups and lies, and He knew what I was *really* craving. It went far beyond the physical taste.

Bill knew I'd been hiding cheese curls again. I knew he knew, and the embarrassment went deep in my soul. My mind was made up. "Bill, will you help me with this?"

"You mean with the septic tank absorbers?"

"Yeah." I said, leaning into him.

"How can I help?"

"Please don't buy me cheese curls anymore."

"So, this is my fault?" he asked.

"No, it's all mine. But that would help. The rest is up to me and Jesus."

I was finally disgusted enough to fall on my face before the Lord. Finally, the problem was out in the light so those who loved me could help. Conviction had come before, but this time was different. My focus had shifted off my ability to overcome, pardon and punish myself. I decided I had to come clean before my family.

"Boys, your mom has a problem. I'm a cheese curl ..."

"I know, Mom, we found your hiding spot in the pantry," said Kyle. "Just don't buy them anymore."

"You knew?"

"It's okay, Mom, we'll help you," said Jonathan.

We prayed asking God for His grace and power. "Don't beat yourself up about this," said Bill. "This isn't the first, nor will it be the last time we help each other overcome a problem. Go forward. It's over. You'll be alright."

I knew that this love of cheese curls went beyond my taste buds. It was greater than enjoying an occasional snack. It was a symptom of something deeper. I was comforting myself, masking an unrest hidden in my soul. The Lord began to show me that each cheesy-curl wasn't a craving as much as it was a clue of something else. It wasn't eating cheese curls that was the biggest sin as much as it was comforting myself with food instead of the Lord. Plus, sneaking, lying, and self-deception. The appetites of flesh always lead in the wrong direction.

The Bible tells us to "run from sin." That means I shouldn't linger in the snack aisle of the grocery store anymore. No more buying "for the kids." They don't need cheese curls either (back to paring carrots!). And no more lying to myself.

The enemy of our soul looms large when hiding in the shadows. Once I brought the temptation out in the open, out into the light, I could see the crunchy cheese curl was small and powerless. How could this little crisp ever overpower my God?

After my humiliating experience trying to flush floaty cheese curls down the toilet, I experienced a miracle. My appetite changed. I tasted one at my grandson's birthday party and couldn't believe how overly salty it was. I could taste all the chemicals and artificial cheese. *Wow, God, this is amazing.*

All-the-way-through excellence includes how I treat the body He has given me. We can't overcome unhealthy behavior with self-discipline alone. I can slam my fist down on the table and declare, "I *will never* do that again." But that places the emphasis on my will and what I am able to perform. I've learned the secret to overcoming begins with repentance and acknowledging that I've sinned. He has taught me to change my self-determination to surrender and trust, and have faith in the promise that He will give me a way of escape. Instead of "I *will* not..." I pray, "Father, it is my *desire* to walk in obedience to You, to eat healthy, and reach for You instead of food for my emotional comfort."

CHAPTER ELEVEN

God's Kiss of Approval

I've been spoiled over the years with the taste of homegrown tomatoes—big juicy vine-ripened ones that burst their skins with flavor—*REAL* tomatoes—fruit that carries God's kiss of approval!

Supermarket tomatoes may look delicious—red and unblemished—but for the most part they are mealy, hard, and tasteless. Growers aren't paid for flavor; they're paid for the pounds of fruit they can put in a box.[6]

---

[6] How Tomatoes End Up Tasting Blah, https://recipes.howstuffworks.com/food-science/quest-to-fix-grocery-store-tomato.htm

Back in the sixties, my mother bought square-shaped tomatoes They were orangish-red colored tough nuggets that came squeezed into a skinny plastic tray encased in cellophane. Growers picked them green and then gassed them with ethylene to make them turn red. Mother put them on the window sill but they wouldn't ripen—or rot! No self-respecting fruit fly ever attacked one of these. They knew a fake tomato when they saw one.

I found it astonishing that people bought these tasteless square tomatoes. They were an embarrassment to God's original design. My mom was trying to be a good, health-conscious mom. She lovingly added them to our baloney sandwiches, but when she wasn't looking, we'd slip out those imposters and throw them in the trash.

A Farm Girl Is Born

If you told me that this sheltered, suburbanite girl, raised on square tomatoes, would ever give a thought to being an organic gardener, I would have said you're dreaming. When I was growing up, my older brother grew pumpkins in the corner of our backyard, but back then, I wouldn't put my cuticles in the dirt if you paid me.

My life changed when we moved into our farmhouse and I explored my neighbor's organic vegetable garden. It was an entirely new experience for me, and I was fascinated. Soon I had my own subscription to the *Organic Gardener* magazine, and I became a devoted follower.

My new garden sprawled out 150 by 50 feet. We didn't have money for a rototiller, so I turned that gigantic plot of land *by hand*. Removing rocks and weeds was a challenge, but I learned how to control the weeds using compost, straw, and newspapers. On very hot days, I'd often wear my bathing suit and work under the sprinkler to keep cool.

I read about the importance of feeding your plants, so I purchased a large galvanized garbage can and set it in the center of the garden to manufacture Marji's Miracle Manure Tea.

First, I collected sheep and cow manure from a nearby farmer's barn and filled the garbage can one-third full. Then I topped it off with water. It took about two weeks, stirring daily, to reach perfection. I carefully ladled the pungent black 'tea' alongside the plants. My plants slurped it up and thanked me by producing the sweetest, most abundant crop of tomatoes.

My faith grew through the principles I employed while gardening. I learned about the importance of feeding and tending my faith, and about making sure there were no nibbling enemies to spoil the vines. It was a good time to think about the Bible verses I'd memorized. "The Lord watches over you ... the Lord is the shade at your right hand ... The Lord will keep you from all harm ... He will watch over your coming and going both now and forevermore ..." (from Psalm 121:5-8).

Wait! What's That Thing?

One day, I saw the chickens having a tug-a-war with something fat and green. I forgot about it until the next morning when I discovered some strange dropping on the leaves of my tomato plants. I cautiously separated the leaves to look for the intruder.

What's that? The *thing* was the size of my forefinger! It had a horn at the end of its—head? —rear? I leaned in for a closer look and I could actually *hear* it *chewing*. It reared up and began bobbing in the air like it was warning me. I almost fell off my stool.

That's what the chickens were fighting over!

The thing totally grossed me out. Meanwhile, the chickens huddled nearby watching my every move. The slimy beast kept chomping while I broke off the branch and tossed it to the chickens. They went wild. I think Queen Matilda ended up with the prize.

All the rest of that day, any time I thought about that big fat green thing, I got the shivers.

That night, just as I was about to fall into a deep sleep, I slid my hand under my pillow and accidentally grabbed my finger. "TOMATO WORM!" I shrieked.

My husband flew off the bed. I swear he didn't come down from the ceiling for ten minutes—Poor guy nearly had a heart attack. Bill threatened to make me wear mittens to bed the next night!

After that, I let my chickens run free in the garden. They helped me keep those intruders at bay. I always wondered if that's where Dr. Seuss got his idea for the book, "*Green* Eggs and Ham."

Hungry Hearts

Abundant crops require good soil. I had a huge compost pile that I nurtured all year, turning it and adding leaves, manure, and grass clippings. The earthworms loved it, too. In the spring, I'd work the compost and worms into my garden making the soil rich and loamy.

The Bible talks about various types of ground in the Parable of the Sower. Actually, the parable has little emphasis on the sower or the seed. It's about the types of soil or heart of the _listener_. The "good ground" mentioned in the parable represents the heart of a _noble and good listener who keeps_ God's word and bears abundant fruit with _patience._

A key element in achieving all-the-way-through excellence can be found in the Greek definition of the word "keeps," _Tereo._ It means _the act of watching over, guarding, maintaining, or preserving._ Figuratively, it means _to spiritually guard (watch), and keep intact._ Dictionary definitions include: _to be faithful to, to tend (as in a garden) to persist in doing and concerning oneself about._ [7]

Proverbs 4:23 says, "Above all else, _guard_ your heart, for everything you do flows from it" (NIV). The New Living Translation says, "...for it determines the course of your life." In other words, "Keep your heart clean before the Lord, guard against the intruders of doubt and unbelief, and be patient with God's process." This is the recipe for growing fruit with God's kiss of approval.

Small Beginnings

Considering how vulnerable plants are at the beginning, reminds me of my small beginnings in the world of ministry. I started writing songs shortly after coming to Christ. I only sang in the privacy of my living room or with the congregation at church. One day I received a phone call from a nearby church asking me

---

[7] Thayer's Greek Lexicon, https://biblehub.com/greek/5083.htm

to come to sing and share my testimony. I couldn't figure out how they even knew I sang.

I didn't grow up in church so I had no idea what to do. I'd memorized dozens of Bible verses by putting them to music, but I had no experience with public speaking. All I had was the guitar my dad gave me when I turned sixteen, the singing voice I inherited from my grandmother, and the love of Jesus growing in my heart.

"What should I do, Bill? I'm not trained. I didn't even go to college."

"Just be yourself. Those things don't matter if you've got the gift."

I wasn't convinced I had *any* gift, but Bill seemed to have enough confidence for the both of us, so I accepted the invitation.

The church was a combination of two congregations, one Methodist, and the other Presbyterian. They joined their services in the summer months when attendance lagged. When I arrived, the minister greeted me harshly with, "Where do you go to church?" Intimidated by his brusqueness, I pointed in a vague direction and muttered the name of my church.

"Why do you go there? We're closer!" he bellowed.

Meekly, I replied. "Because I get good Gospel there."

He stiffened. "Well, you won't get good Gospel here!"

I was speechless. *Isn't that what a church is for?*

As I watched him saunter off, his white bucks scuffing the back hem of his robes, I remembered snippets of verses I'd put to music: *I am His child … He is with me … greater is He that is in me.* Courage rose in my heart, and I had the strange sense God *meant* for me to be there. Still, I wished for the security of my farmhouse where there were no expectations and I could sing to the admiring audience of One.

The pastor sauntered up to the podium. "We have something unusual today. A housewife from Rush, Marji Stevens, is going to sing and share." The pastor gestured in my direction. I smiled nervously and walked to the front of the church and strapped on my guitar.

"Thank you for inviting me. My name is … well, you already know that." I giggled and cleared my throat. "I asked Jesus Christ to come and live in my heart. Sometimes in the morning when I have peace and quiet to read my Bible and pray, I feel inspired to write a song." I softly started to strum my guitar. "This is a song I wrote recently. I hope you enjoy it."

The congregation appeared somewhat uncomfortable. First of all, why is a *woman* with a *guitar* standing up in front in our church? She's not *clergy* … and where's the choir? While I sang and shared my faith, the people seemed divided into three groups. Some looked at me as if they wanted to do me serious bodily harm. Others stared at me like I was speaking a foreign language. The third group had an open, hungry look on their faces. After the service, the last group crowded around me. One man said, "You don't know how long we've waited to hear that in this church." The pastor exited the back door without saying a word.

That invitation resulted in another, and another until I was regularly invited to churches of all denominations. In the beginning, I introduced myself as "the untrained" until the Holy Spirit corrected me one day. He said, "What do you call spending time with Me in the privacy of your living room? Am I not training you?" Just as my *Organic Gardener* magazine taught me how to garden, the Lord was teaching me through His Word. He was cultivating the soil of my heart, mulching it to grow the seed of His Word and protecting my plants from intruders. God Himself was training me.

Be Yourself

The Lord Jesus was teaching me how to "keep" my heart free from the invasive "tomato worms" of discouragement, and doubt. The rocks, thorns, and weeds mentioned in the Parable of the Sower come in many forms. For example, I auditioned to sing in a professional choir in my city. Since I never learned to read music, I sang what I believed to be the accurate rendition of the Lord's Prayer. A quarter of the way through, the choral director slammed his hands down on the piano keys and barked, "Whoever told you that you could sing?" He got up and left the room.

I was devastated. First, nobody had ever treated me so rudely, and second, the devil used that statement to reinforce the rocky fears in my heart that having a music ministry was just a vain imagination—*I knew it, I'm no good. The trained professional told me so—God hasn't called me to this. It's just my imagination.*

While I was preparing dinner that evening, the director's words rolled over and over in my mind. I couldn't hold back the tears. My son came into the kitchen, saw me crying and asked what was wrong. He leaned against the kitchen counter and listened intently. When I was finished, he paused for a few minutes then said, "Mom—you either trust God or you don't."

I stared at him. It felt like a touch from heaven. I put down what I was doing and gave him a big hug. "You amaze me sometimes. Are you really only twelve years old?"

"Mom, you always tell ME to be myself—that means you, too."

I hugged him again and kissed him on the cheek, "You're a good son, Jonathan. You said exactly what God wanted me to hear."

So many lasting spiritual lessons came from this gardening adventure. But in the process, I learned how to trust the Holy Spirit to show me how to guard the garden of my heart, to keep the ground soft and free of rocks and weeds, and to carefully choose only seeds of excellence, with the ultimate goal to one day hear Him say, "Well done faithful servant. You have grown fruit with My kiss of approval."

CHAPTER TWELVE

An Unwelcome Guest

My favorite season is fall when the temperature dips brisk and the trees turn into a kaleidoscope of color. Once the trees start to deposit their leaves on the ground, we have to start the task of raking. My mother says I should have the boys do it, but at their ages, to rake is to pile, and to pile is to dive. Personally, I pray for a big wind.

Fall also brings an influx of critters hunting for a home out of the cold. No matter how we patch and fill, those blasted, munching murines find their way in. One year, we gave permission to the local fire department to burn down our dilapidated hay barn for training purposes. Little did we realize when we approved this venture that all the critters that lived in that old barn would stampede to our house like illegal aliens searching for the land of plenty. Our two, scruffy tom cats were superior mousers, but even they had their limits of what they could catch and eat. I had no idea what we were in for.

Bill and the boys stay busy a good deal of late summer and fall splitting and stacking wood for the winter. I fix my attention on our food supply. I dehydrate, can, and freeze as if the grocery stores are going out of business. I filled the pantry with tomatoes, peaches, applesauce, pickles, vegetables, jams, braided onions, and butternut squash. That primitive four-by-seven-foot room transforms into a gold mine of goodness for the family—and the mice. No matter how careful I am, if the slightest stickiness is left on the canning jars, they're sure to find it.

Alien Invasion

Sitting with my Bible at the kitchen table one morning, out of the corner of my eye I saw something streak across the floor and under my chair. I jerked my feet up as fast as I could and nervously scanned the kitchen. *What was that?* A tingle of shivers ran up my spine. Our cats were sound asleep by the wood stove, bellies still swollen from the previous night's hunting. *If it wasn't a cat, what was it?*

I tried to return to my Bible study, but couldn't concentrate. I kept wondering what I'd seen move across the kitchen floor. I remembered an incident years ago. I was nursing Jonathan late at night in our bedroom when I heard loud sniffing coming from the door to the crawlspace next to me.

"BILL, there's a monster gonna eat my baby."

Still glued to his pillow, all I heard was, "You'll be okay. It can wait 'till morning."

It turned out to be a pregnant raccoon that had crawled into our attic through a hole in the roof looking for a place to have her babies.

Oh Lord, what went under my chair? My mind raced back to the time a garden snake crawled out of a crack in the floor of the bathroom. Bill was at work, and the boys were too little to help. I ran for the snow shovel and poked at the snake until it attacked the shovel. Fortunately, the window was open and we had no screens—out it went. I had the creepy crawlies for days.

Then there was the time the cat had a mouse cornered behind a cabinet outside our bedroom door. She stared at that cabinet for hours. I knew she was hunting a mouse, but I was too tired to deal with it. I set a trap and went to bed. Later that night, I was awakened by the cat scurrying across the bedroom floor. I was about to roll over and ignore the whole ordeal until I felt tiny, pointy feet run across my forehead!

"BILL ...I just ..."

"You're okay, it can wait 'til morning."

Oh, the Horror …

Our living room is the sunniest room in the house. It's where I grow my prized African violets. I'd been training one particular beauty all year for a garden show in the fall. The horrid scene that greeted me brought instant tears. All the velvety leaves I'd carefully trained into a perfect nosegay arrangement lay broken and scattered on the table. I concluded the boys had been playing football in the house again.

"They're in trouble NOW!" I stomped over to the front door and yelled, "Boys, come in the house—RIGHT AWAY!"

They observed my angry, tear-streaked face, dropped what they were doing, and ran to the door.

"What's the matter, Mom?" Kyle asked.

"Matter?" Jon echoed.

I led them into the living room and pointed to the smashed violet. "THAT! THAT'S WHAT'S THE MATTER! How many times have I told you—NO football in the house!"

The boys started jumping up and down vigorously denying they had any part in it. Jon stomped his foot. "Di-nent do it, Mom." He scowled at the unjust accusation.

I was indignant. How could they stand there, in front of the evidence, and deny it? "That's it? Go to your rooms and don't come out until you are ready to tell me the truth."

Jon protested loudly as I hustled them both upstairs. "Di-nent do it!" he yelled. Kyle drooped his shoulders and followed his brother.

I returned to the living room and tenderly picked up the broken leaves. For a fleeting moment I imagined I could somehow reattach them. I noticed something unusual on the floor. I bent over to examine what looked like a *huge* mouse dropping. A trail of them led behind the couch where my baby African violets grow under lights. What a mess! Smashed leaves everywhere. Dug up plants lay in ruins. It didn't take the deductive reasoning of Sherlock Holmes to solve this crime—a King Kong mouse got in the house.

I called the boys. Their bedroom doors squeaked open. "Come down here, please. I want to talk to you." They scrambled down the stairs and I led them into the living room to see what I found. "Boys, I think I know what happened, and I'm sorry I blamed you before I had the facts. This is the job of a giant mouse."

Kyle bent down to examine the droppings. His eyes went wide. "Uh, Mom, those aren't mouse droppings. That's a RAT!"

The "R" word had never been mentioned in this house. "Oh NO!" I gasped. Then it dawned on me, "That must be what I saw run under my chair yesterday!"

"Under your *CHAIR*!" exclaimed Kyle.

I shuddered in remembrance. "Yes, I was reading a book and out of the corner of my eye I saw something streak across the floor and under my chair."

Kyle wrinkled up his nose and frowned. "The rat must have been hunting for a home after the barn burned down. Where was Babe?"

I pointed to the mound of yarn in the middle of the living room, "Guess."

We sat down on the couch to talk. "Guys, I'm so sorry. I feel terrible about how quickly I accused you."

Kyle patted me softly on the shoulder. "It's okay, Mom. You didn't know."

Five-year-old Jon, on the other hand, wasn't so quick to

forgive my transgression. He reminded me righteously, "Told you, Mom."

But where was the rat now? It had been digging in the dirt around the plants probably trying to escape, but did it succeed another way?

Now I stomped my foot! "Bill, I've put up with mice by the droves, snakes in the bathroom, raccoons in the attic, but there is NOWAY I'm putting up with a RAT."

Bill assured me I was okay and promised to take care of it.

"I know," I mumbled. "In the morning."

That night, Bill fell asleep on his way down to the pillow. I lay there staring at the ceiling when Kyle tip-toed into our bedroom. "Dad, don't wake Mom, but …"

I shot straight up in bed. "But what? What's the matter? What's going on?"

"I heard something in the kitchen and went to see what it was. Babe has the rat cornered by the garbage can."

"I'll get my shotgun," Bill said.

"Don't do THAT! You'll shoot a hole in the house," I protested.

"Then the rat can get out," he said. "You stay here."

I waited for the shotgun blast. Fortunately, a hole in the house wasn't necessary because Babe had already killed it.

"Babe's a hero!" Jon yelled up the stairs.

Thankfully, I was spared the details of where they disposed of our un-welcomed guest. I couldn't help feeling a swell of fondness for good-old Babe. She didn't prevent the crime, but at least she helped the criminal get his just punishment.

In my journal that day I wrote:

"Our unwelcome guest served as a great object lesson. I guess every critter—great and small—can be used by God on my journey to all-the-way-through excellence. I learned today that love doesn't make a judgement until all the facts are in. From now on, when my boys tell me they "di-nint do it," I need to believe they are innocent *until* proven guilty."

104

CHAPTER THIRTEEN

Moss Management and Water Distribution

For years I've traipsed over fields and streams, through woods and brush, following my husband on his nature walks. Bill never cared to follow the path; he wanted to forge his own. Okay, but Bill was much taller than me. He stood at 6'4" while I am only 5'4". When tromping merrily through tall grass and weeds, I was left at a clear disadvantage. Frankly, I had a different idea about taking a walk in the woods with my honey. I'd go with expectations of a pause, a kiss, a picking a wildflower. We had those moments, but most of the time while I thought about romance, Bill had his mind on buck-scrapes and deer droppings. He always had a knack for leading me to discover fascinating signs of life.

"You can tell the deer slept here last night," he said, pointing toward the fields. "After bedding down here, they traveled north in that direction."

Eventually, I learned to pick out the signs myself. I took a walk with a girlfriend one day, and proudly pointed out the different droppings along the way. She wasn't impressed, "What's all this fascination with animal poop?" she remarked. I guess some knowledge isn't for everyone.

I met a friend who had the gift of sight like Bill—only it didn't come from tromping through fields. Walter couldn't walk through fields like my husband could, but he opened my eyes to levels of intimacy with the Lord I didn't know were possible. My heart was drawn to him at a church gathering, because he had cerebral palsy like my brother, George. We became instant friends.

Walter had no family and lived alone. He had a remarkably deep walk with the Lord. He spent most of his time in prayer and contemplation. We invited Walter over for dinner one evening and he asked if he could bring his slide projector and show slides.

After dinner, Bill excused himself to correct test papers for school the next day. Walter and I went into the living room to set up the projector.

"When I bring up another slide," he explained. "I want you to study it and tell me if any scripture comes to mind." At first, nothing came to me. Walter continued to coach me with different slides. "What spiritual principle do you see when you look at this picture of a tree?"

I suddenly saw what Walter was trying to teach me. "Well, this one is easy," I remarked. "It makes me think of Psalm 1. If we meditate on the Word of God day and night, our roots are established and we become like a tree firmly planted by rivers of living water."

Walter smiled. "Good," he said, "Psalm 19:1 tells us that the heavens are recounting the glory of God. Day and night His word drips off every leaf and blade all around you. You just have to take the time to ponder what you see and listen to the Holy Spirit."

What Walter shared through those slides started me on a journey that increased my creativity and greatly enriched my devotional life. I began to look beneath the surface of things and hunt for His Word hidden everywhere.

Bryophyta ... Moss

I found an old nature book the perfect size to carry with me. Before this, I took walks just for the purpose of exercise. Now I hunted for the hidden revelations of His Word waiting to be discovered. Time outside became a classroom full of inspiration.

Moss grows everywhere, especially in shaded woods and forests where there is plenty of moisture. The nature book defined moss, or *Bryophyta* as tiny, thread-like rhizoids, *reaching out like trusting fingers* to find nutrients and anchorage.

What a lovely image—trusting fingers reaching out. I felt the Lord's tug on my heart and I immediately thought of Psalm 63: "O God, You are my God; I earnestly search for You. My soul thirsts for you; my whole body longs for you in this parched and weary land where there is no water" (Psalm 63:1 NLT).

I remember a walk I took with a group of women through the woodlands and along the gorge at beautiful Buttermilk Falls in

Ithaca, New York. It's a state park that features a cascading waterfall and river that winds for a couple miles along the steep valley side toward Cayuga Lake. Rock steps, carved out along the water's edge, mark the way to the top of the gorge.

About halfway up, the trail turns into a narrow passage that cuts between the water's edge and a towering wall of shale. We entered an alcove-like room, a secret space, unseen unless you were on the path. A sweet, woodsy scent mixed with the mist that billowed from the foaming waterfall, cascaded into a rocky pool.

The women sat down beside the water to rest, but I was drawn to walk over to the rock precipice on the opposite side. Its jagged edges glistened with mist from the waterfall. Spongy, seedless plants in every spectrum of green, clung along the brittle grooves. The mossy plants branched haphazardly, absorbing the heavy mist that hung in the air. I discovered I barely needed to touch the moss and it would release a delightful trickle of water. *How wonderful—trusting fingers reaching out—finding all they need.*

I could hear the women joking about how old and out of shape the climb made them feel, and how the mist ruined their hair. My thoughts were in a different place. I knew the Lord was focusing my attention on the moss and I wanted to soak up every detail.

We finished our walk in the late afternoon and had a couple of hours of free time before dinner. I decided to write about my experience. As I reached for my journal, I sensed the Lord speaking to me.

"I want *you* to be like that moss."

In my mind, I was back in that beautiful secret alcove and I heard Him whisper: "My people are meant to grow like tender moss clinging to the Rock, saturated with Living Water, and full of the fragrances of Heaven. I want my children to be so full of My

Spirit that the witness of their lives will release with the slightest touch."

A plant full of water doesn't have to *try* to be wet. It's wet because it's saturated with water. That moss couldn't be any other way if it tried. The water is not *of* the plant it is *of* the waterfall. The moss on the shale was filled with the same water that misted the air, filled the pool, and beaded on my jacket. The waterfall impacted everything that came near it.

I knew this was another example of the life of a virtuous woman. My journal entry that day was: "The active quality of excellence is an expression of what you're filled with."

The next time I'm on an airplane, and someone asks me what line of work I'm in, instead of saying, "The ministry," I think I should say: "Moss Management and Water Distribution. How about you?" That's sure to spark conversation.

The life of forests largely depends on their ability to maintain moisture from the individual mosses and plants they shelter. In a similar manner, the life of Christ's church depends on the water of life retained and released by its members.

This reminds me of the Samaritan woman who went to get water at the well and found Jesus sitting there. Hesitantly, she approached Him, not knowing who He was and who asked her for a drink. The revelation of His identity grew the longer they spoke. Soon the woman was declaring her new-found joy to others. Arriving empty, she left full of living water. She came to the well looking for a temporary supply, but Jesus filled her with His *everlasting* supply. She had discovered the source of life.

We're walking through the fields of life with an adventuresome outdoorsman, and He used Walter to open my eyes to the wonder of His world. Walter couldn't walk through the fields like my husband, but he taught me how to discover God's secrets hidden in the beauty of nature. The Lord wants us to have the same anticipation of surprise when we follow Him, for He is the Way, the Truth and will always lead us to Life.

My journal entry that day read:

> "I love how God's Word drips off every leaf and blade. I need only to take the time to look and listen to the Holy Spirit. He is delighted to teach us how to live like moss—nestled in the Rock, saturated with His Living Water, and ready to serve His purpose."

CHAPTER FOURTEEN

A Ticket and A Treasure

It's interesting to imagine what kind of parables Jesus would teach today if He were with us in the flesh. Jesus used practical illustrations taken from the ordinary culture of the times to get the attention of the people.

I conducted a ladies' retreat one early summer weekend on Canandaigua Lake in Upstate New York. The sunshine reflecting on the calm blue-green water provided a perfect day. Little did I know a real-life parable was about to capture our attention.

There's nothing quite like a fresh testimony to boost your teaching and create an inspired moment of relevance. As my dad always said, "Everything that happens in life is just another funny story to tell." However, I heartily agree with whoever uttered: "There is usually a test *and a moan* in every test-i-mony?"

During our morning session, I taught about the power and authority of God's Word and the importance of obedience. I also discussed the peace of God and how the Holy Spirit uses the inner witness of peace to guide us when making decisions. After lunch, the women had time to enjoy being outside in such a beautiful location.

A few of the women decided to use the center's rowboats. That's what I also hoped to do, but by the time I got to the dock all the rowboats were taken. The only craft remaining was a dinky paddle boat.

The girls in the rowboats were grouped together not far from shore. On an impulse, another lady and I climbed into the  paddle boat and headed out to join the others.

The gals in the rowboats saw us peddling their way and began to cheer us on. From across the lake, a large motorboat came speeding in our direction. It turned out to be the sheriff's patrol boat. I assumed he was coming to make sure we were all right. Everyone waved as the officer cut his engines and drifted towards us.

Our ridiculous paddle boat rocked furiously in his wake. "Do you women have your life jackets?" he inquired. Everyone quickly waved them in the air—everyone, that is, except us.

"Ladies, do you have your life vests?" he barked.

I had no experience with lakes and boats and never gave life vests a thought. "Sorry, officer, no, sir, we don't."

Much to my surprise, he wasn't the least bit impressed with our submissive tone. Instead, he produced a little black book and began to write. "I'm giving you each a ticket for breaking the law."

I gasped. "A ticket? But officer, we're in a *paddle boat*!"

He shook his head, "Let me see your driver's license."

"But sir, we're in a *paddle boat!* Who takes a purse in a *p-a-d-d-l-e boat*."

"That will cost each of you $35."

At first, I was outraged. *Why did he have to be so gruff and mean? Couldn't he have given us a break? We were polite.*

I held onto the side of his boat so we wouldn't drift apart and watched him fill out the citations. *This just isn't fair.* The officer tore the tickets from his book and leaned over the side of the boat to hand them to me. That's when I saw a change in him. The scowl on his face softened. He looked me in the eyes and said, "Listen, if you've ever pulled a drowning victim's body from the bottom of this lake, you would appreciate why all water safety violators are ticketed. Next time, learn the laws before you head out. Consider this a wake-up call to protect your lives and property." He patted my hand, "Have a good day."

His sudden kindness and pat on the hand dispelled my anger.

Everyone rowed back to the dock in silence. The women were upset. "That's so unfair." "I can't believe he gave you a ticket." One lady even cried, "We should protest in front of the town hall."

"Thanks," I said. "But, no matter how you cut it, it's my fault for not taking the time to learn the safety laws before getting in that boat. There are always consequences when we break the rules. Ignorance is never an excuse."

Propelled By Peace

If I stopped to test my inner peace before jumping in that paddleboat, would I have sensed the Lord's warning to wear a life vest? Or, did He allow this to highlight our morning discussion? Either way, the lessons are rich.

Our family has an uncontested rule: *If you don't feel peace about something—don't do it.* I remember the time the four of us got dressed up and paraded to the car for a special outing.

However, when Bill sat behind the steering wheel, he didn't start the car.

The kids protested. "What's the matter, Dad? Come on, let's go."

My heart sank because I knew what was happening. Bill didn't feel peace. Sure enough, after a long silence, Bill said, "Sorry family, we're not going. For some reason, I don't feel peace." We all simultaneously groaned. The kids dragged themselves into the house, complaining that now they had nothing to do.

"Gee, Moooom, now what are we going to do today...I r-e-a-l-l-y wanted to go," whined Jon.

"I know, but we have to pay attention when we don't feel peaceful about something. It's the Lord's way of protecting us. It's God's way of saying 'stop.' We need to listen. You can be thankful you have a father who listens to the Holy Spirit."

That rule saved our son's life one day. Kyle was traveling home the usual route after work, but when he got to his turn, he said he suddenly felt very unpeaceful. "Mom, it was so weird. I had no peace about going down that road. I always go that way! But I decided to take the next street." We found out later there a fatal accident had just occurred at the end of that road. A truck plowed into a passenger car driven by a teenage boy. The young man, my son's age, was killed. Had Kyle not listened to that inner witness and taken another route, he could have been that young man. Or, he might have witnessed a tragic scene hard to forget.

In Deuteronomy, we are told that God wasn't pleased with the Israelites when they rushed into battle (1:42-45). He tried to tell them not to fight, but they didn't listen. Clothed only with their good intentions, they hastened to do what seemed perfectly reasonable to them. It was, of course, a disaster. Instead of returning as God's victorious army, they were stung by defeat and humiliation, as if chased by bees.

Jesus used stories called parables to illustrate an important point. He is the *author* and *finisher* of our faith. He knows engaging stories about people and real-life situations help us grasp and remember deep spiritual principles. That evening I talked about my brush with the law. The women got a good laugh as well as a parable-like illustration about obedience to God's laws.

As it turns out, that $35 was money well spent just to have another funny story to tell. No matter how many times I share this story I always get the same response: "*What?* You got a ticket in a *paddle boat*? Only you, Marj."

My journal entry that day read:
"I got a ticket *and a treasure*. A ticket because I broke the safety boating laws on Canandaigua Lake; the treasure because I have another funny story to tell. It was a reminder of how much He loves us and wants to keep us safe. Lord, please help me be More sensitive when Your Holy Spirit ruffles my peace. Amen."

116

CHAPTER FIFTEEN

The Dody Box

I remember as a child the day a large UPS truck rumbled up the driveway. Everyone stopped what they were doing and scrambled to see who the package was for.

"It's for me! It's a Dody box." I shrieked. "Dody sent me a prize!" Nothing more wonderful could happen in this ten-year-old's day.

I tore open the cardboard box which concealed another box wrapped in elegant gold foil paper tied with a deep burgundy satin ribbon. I carefully peeled back each piece of tape, draped the regal ribbon over my shoulders, and lifted the lid on the box. Vibrant splashes of multi-colored tissue paper cushioned each treasure tucked inside. It was like a glowing flower garden in a box.

Aunt Dody always presented her surprise packages with style and flare. I think it was impossible for her to ever be ordinary. These were her "just because" gifts. Her tokens of love. They usually came nowhere near a holiday and represented the love she had for her family.

To my delight, I found some perfume and a brightly colored silk scarf that I swirled in the air and let drape over my shoulders. Next, I found some jewelry and a tiny little gold compact encased in a black, sequined velvet sleeve. These were not gifts for a little girl, but that's exactly what made the treasures so wonderful.

As I came to the bottom of the box, I found something larger than all the other packages. "A music box! I can't believe Aunt Dody sent me a music box!" I carefully wound the key and out streamed "Some Enchanted Evening." How did Dody know that I'd secretly wished for a music box?

My Aunt Dody was an example of thoughtfulness and generosity. I wanted to grow up to be as giving and creative as she was. The very fact that Dody lived in New York City held a certain mystique for me as a young girl. Dody never married. She only had a third-grade education, but she worked her way up to being the vice president of the Westchester Country Club in Rye, New York. She selflessly gave herself to her job and to the people she served. Dody was loved by everyone. People showered her with extraordinary gifts to express their admiration and gratitude for her service. She received more gifts than any one person could ever enjoy. Several times a year, Dody gathered up an assortment of these treasures, wrapped them with her Dody-flare and sent them to her family.

Dody was a heavy-set, buxom woman. I can remember looking

up at her chest as a small child and wondering how anyone could have that much out front and not fall forward. Her cleavage appeared to start directly under her chin. I watched her make hankies disappear down there a number of times and idly wondered what else she could hide if she wanted to. A few times my brother and I got our faces smothered in one of her gigantic hugs and came up gulping for air.

Her silver, blue-gray hair was kept in a French twist—often to one side making room for a burst of fresh flowers. Her soft, smiling blue eyes always sparkled as if she had a wealth of fun ideas just waiting to pop out. Dody was also known for her charm bracelets. She wore several on each wrist. You could hear the soft jingle of her bracelets announcing her entrance into a room. I can remember the feeling of excitement every time I heard that sound. *Here she comes!*

The many gifts of love Dody sent over the years always made me feel loved and special. They were completely *unexpected* acts of kindness and generosity.

Hesed—Love in Action

One of the Hebrew words for 'love' is *hesed*. It's difficult to translate this word into English, but is often explained as "completely undeserved kindness and generosity."[8] One of my favorite Scriptures is: "Though the mountains be shaken, and the hills be removed, *yet my unfailing love* (*hesed*) for you will not be shaken" (Isaiah 54:10). *Hesed* is not just a feeling, but an action. It's God's love sent from heaven that thoroughly surprises and

---

[8] John Oswalt's definition. The Meaning of Hesed: Hebrew for Love. By Avital Snow. https://firmisrael.org/learn/the-meaning-of-hesed-hebrew-for-love/

delights us, like 'Dody boxes' sent from Heaven. It's not a romantic love, it's a faithful, reliable love. Most importantly, *hesed* is the *unfailing love* God has for us.

It wasn't until my early twenties that I understood that the many blessings in my life were God wooing me to Himself. The song, "Your Kindness," by Leslie Ann Phillips, expresses it so well. The chorus is: "It's Your kindness that leads us to repentance, O Lord. Knowing that You love us, no matter what we do, makes us want to love You, too..." We love God because He first loved us. (1 John 4:19) That's God's *hesed* - His acts of grace and mercy completely undeserved.

The Sweetest Surprise

During my sons' growth spurts, it was difficult to afford to buy two pairs of sneakers and new jeans all at once. I had to spread out the cost over several paychecks. We had to curb every unnecessary expenditure in order to keep shoes on their ever-lengthening feet. Needless to say, perfume for Mom was not considered a necessity. When I used the last drop of my perfume, I knew it would be quite a while before I got a fresh supply. Though I secretly wished for more, I never said anything.

After ministering in a church in Pennsylvania, a woman hesitantly approached me with both hands behind her back. "Excuse me, Marji. Do you accept presents? An idea has been gnawing at me for the last month and I feel I have to give this to you." She shyly presented me with a little box. "Someone gave this to me, but the minute I opened it, I knew it was not meant for me. I feel the Lord intends for you to have it."

I opened the box and buried beneath rainbow tissue paper was a little bottle of … "Perfume! You have no idea what this means to me," I exclaimed. "Mine is all gone. The Lord heard the longing of my heart!"

"I knew it," she said. Tears glistened in her eyes as she responded with a generous hug. Through her unexpected act of kindness, the Lord said to me, "Here is a little token of My love." My husband had never cared for perfume. He said that most of them smelled like bug spray and mothballs. But this perfume he *loved*. I wore it daily until it was gone. When I tried to buy more, no matter where I looked, no one had ever heard of it.

A similar thing happened when my husband and sons *forgot* Mother's Day for the first time. It hurt my feelings. I found myself rehearsing all the reasons why they *should* have remembered. When they finally realized what had happened, I was smothered with hugs and kisses. A few days later, I left on a trip to minister at a women's retreat. After the morning session, a lady bobbed up in front of me and said, "Here!" She gleefully plopped a package in my hands. "The Lord told me to get this for you a week ago." Then she bounced away, disappearing before I could thank her.

I opened the box and found a little pink mug with the inscription: "Love's a special gift you give away every single day you live," and on the back it said: "Happy Mother's Day!" My sheer amazement moved me to tears. "Oh, how wonderful You are, Lord. You didn't forget me on Mother's Day!"

Alone in my room that evening the Lord gave me a little worship song:

It's the way that You love me, Lord,
Keeps me running to be next to You.
It's the way that You love me, Lord,
Makes the joy of my life loving You.

I wasn't journaling during the years when Dody was living, but her influence filled my journals in later years. God's excellence, grown in our hearts, will always produce the fruit of unselfish, loving generosity. The honored practice of giving an unexpected token of love, nowhere near a holiday, continues in my house to this day. We call them "Just Because" presents—just because I love you.

God's love tokens and caresses are the sweetest. There isn't anything more wonderful that can happen to our day than a touch of *hesed*.

Dody passed away by the time I was a young mother, but my home still displays the beautiful gifts she sent over the years. Because of her I frequently approach tasks with the thought: "How can I add a Dody flare?"

CHAPTER SIXTEEN

Philip

The multiple roofs of the county home set an ominous silhouette against the city. Statues of gargoyles and dragons resided high up in the eaves. A cloud of suffering seemed to hover over that place. It was home to hundreds of needy souls. Some were too poor for a nursing home. Some needed long-term chronic care, and many others people wanted to forget. Philip lived there.

I first visited the county home with a group of women from my church. Christmas brought out the usual influx of carolers from all sorts of organizations. The entire scene depressed me. All I thought about were the months between January and March when the sun seldom shines in Western New York, and few ever visit. I was determined to return, but nowhere near a holiday.

During this first caroling visit, I met Philip. He was a small, fragile, hunch-backed man reduced to skin and bones. His head twisted permanently to one side and he walked painfully bent over; a white towel draped over his shoulder. I couldn't take my eyes off him. He exuded the joy of the Lord despite his disabilities. When the women began to sing, Philip started to rock back and forth, groaning softly. He raised his hands in the air and tears began streaming down his face.

In the days following our visit, I couldn't stop thinking about Philip. A few months after Christmas I returned to visit him. Even though months had passed, he remembered me. "How about a song, Philip? May I sing to you?" He immediately raised his hands and began to cry and give thanks.

Philip enjoyed my singing, and always asked for more. Every once in a while, the music would inspire him and he'd begin to quote entire sections of scripture. I'd stop and listen. I flowed in and out of worship for over an hour. On one occasion, I dared to ask Philip how he came to live there. He said when he was sixteen, he was taking a walk in the woods one day and stopped to rededicate his life to the Lord. He stopped to cry and express thanks. After wiping his tears with his towel, he continued. "I asked God, what He wanted to do with my life." Without hesitation he added, "And He sent me here."

I was stunned. Philip gave no explanation concerning the disability that qualified him for the county home. He only expressed his total surrender to the will of God. "My life is His," he said. "Whatever He wants for me is fine."

When I stepped out of that building, I took a deep breath of fresh air. A hush of reverence lingered in my spirit. Philip had lived almost his entire life in that place. I shuddered at the thought of being confined in one building with little to no exposure to the outside world. I couldn't imagine not having a car and the freedom to go where I wanted to go. *Lord, how does he do it with such joy?* His words rolled over and over in my thoughts ... *"My life is His. Whatever He wants for me is fine."* I knew I'd been introduced to one of God's treasures; and the message of Philip's life brought deep conviction. Though I cherished meeting him, I didn't like that place. I found the sadness too suffocating, and determined not to go again.

More than a year went by when my friend and I were driving home after a ministry engagement. She needed to stop for a few minutes at the county home. I didn't want to go inside so I agreed to wait in the car. The day was warm and sunny. I rolled down my window and viewed the park-like surroundings. An unusual thought suddenly crossed my mind, "Go sing to the man on the park bench." Way at the back of the expansive lawn, under the shade of a large tree, I could see a man sitting on a bench.

I imagined myself walking up to that man saying, "Hello there, stranger sitting on the bench, I'm here to serenade you." *I can't do that. That's embarrassing. What would people think?*

The Lord read my thoughts and He said, "What is more important to you, the opinion of man or being obedient to Me?"

I gulped. "Okay, Lord, I'll just wait until my friend comes back, and we'll go together."

"Do you need an audience to do My will?" came the reply.

With some hesitancy still in my heart, I left the guitar in the car and started walking trying to look as if taking a stroll. It wasn't until I came closer that I dared to look directly at the man. That's when I saw the white towel draped over his shoulder.

"Philip? Is that you?"

He immediately began to cry and give thanks.

"Philip, do you remember me?"

He lifted up his hands. "I've been waiting for you," he said. "The Lord told me you were coming today."

Stunned, I said I'd be right back. I ran to the car to get my guitar. *I DID hear You, Lord! Oh, thank you, thank you.* I hurried back as fast as I could. Under the tree, with the roar of the city behind us, I played my guitar and sang to Philip as he cried and worshiped the Lord. It was a tender moment in a very harsh world.

I don't know if Philip held a vision in his heart that ever was fulfilled, or if he dreamed of perhaps a different home. If he did, he never mentioned it. He just spoke of trust and thankfulness.

Philip has gone on to be with the Lord. He was a treasure undiscovered by most. Few knew he ever lived. The world would probably say that Philip's life was a failure. He never had his picture in the newspaper. No one ever invited him to speak at an event or sit on a committee. Philip never owned a suit or a car, or had a career. He wasn't concerned about developing his self-esteem or fulfilling some ambition. All he had was a white towel to blot his tears, and a heart that loved the Lord.

"... For I was hungry and you gave Me food, I was thirsty and you gave Me drink, I was a stranger and you welcomed Me in; I was naked and you clothed Me; I was sick and you visited Me; I was in prison and you came to Me. ... Assuredly, I say to you, inasmuch as you did it to one of the least of these My brethren, you did it to Me." (Matthew 25:35-36, 40 NKJV)

CHAPTER SEVENTEEN

The Hand of Special Grace

One of my earliest invitations to sing and share was at a Catholic charismatic prayer meeting. It was there that I met Janet. I was drawn by her warm and friendly demeanor. During refreshments, I learned that Janet had spent 20 years in a convent and now worked with cerebral palsy adults at the Al Sigl Center in Rochester.

"This is amazing," I exclaimed. "My brother, George, has cerebral palsy. * For years he's gone to Al Sigl for physical therapy—you might even know him."

Janet's face softened. "Would you ever be interested in coming to minister to my group?"

A shiver ran up my spine. "Oh, I'd love to."

We poured ourselves a cup of coffee and sat down. "My daughter has a mild case of cerebral palsy," Janet said. "Tell me about your brother."

"Well, George's handicap is complicated by the fact that he's deaf and partially blind. But he has amazing determination to be independent. It's truly remarkable what he's been able to accomplish. I've never met anyone as joyful as my brother."

"How old were you when George was born?" she asked.

"Ten."

Janet thoughtfully ran her finger around the rim of her coffee cup. "Our children were around that age when our daughter was born. They struggled with the sacrifices they had to make, due to the attention required to meet her needs. How did you handle the shift in your family dynamics?"

I had to think for a moment. "The whole family struggled with the adjustments, though we didn't talk about it. It was several years before Mom and Dad knew the full scope of George's disabilities. Dad insisted George was just a late bloomer. My mom had a sister with cerebral palsy so she accepted it before my dad did. Everything we did as a family revolved around what was best for George. I wrestled with resentment as a teenager, but those issues have been resolved since I met the Lord.

"God has used every bit of it. I especially remember something I overheard our babysitter, Mrs. Riker, say. She told my mother that 'God gives *special grace* to those with special needs.' I knew what she meant by special needs, but at the time I had no idea what she meant by *special grace*. I can still see Mrs. Riker sitting in our living room reading her Bible. I'd never seen anyone read a Bible before. I loved the crinkly sound the paper of her Bible made when she turned the pages."

"Wow. She was a wise woman," Janet said. "Sounds to me God used Mrs. Riker's comment to help point you to Himself."

"His hand of grace was leading me long before I accepted Him as my Savior. Every time I go through something difficult, I'm reminded to trust His special grace for my special needs."

We parted ways with a date for me to visit her group at Al Sigl Center. I felt sure because of my experience with George, that I would be able to handle the engagement with ease. I was wrong. George's cerebral palsy was mild in comparison to those in Janet's group. Walking into that facility I was immediately overwhelmed by the sights, sounds, and smells. My first instinct was to turn around and leave.

Janet saw me walk in the door and came right over. "We are so excited you are here to sing to us today. I've told them all about you. You can first join us in the cafeteria. Once we're finished eating and back in our room, I'll introduce you. Take as much time as you'd like."

The lunchroom was about 85 degrees and smelled like stale hospital food. Staff members were busy applying bibs and situating the wheel chairs. Some individuals needed help guiding the food to their mouths. Some managed on their own. Some choked and gagged, coughing with every bite. I began to feel queasy inside. *Lord, I can't do this. Please help. I need Your grace, Your power to do this.*

Janet pointed to the chair opposite where she was sitting. "You can sit here with us. I'd like you to meet Gordon. I'll be helping him today."

Gordon was the most limited adult in the class. He was strapped into a high-backed wheelchair. His body was twisted and severely spastic. Completely dependent, Gordon couldn't talk or feed himself. A steady stream of drool trickled from the corner of his mouth, soaking the big bib tied around his neck.

"Open up. Today is sweet potato and chicken." Janet cradled his head in her arms and put the spoon full of baby food up to Gordon's mouth. His body spasmed and his arms jerked out to his sides as he tried to open his mouth. Most of the food streamed out onto the bib as he choked and sputtered with every bite.

Janet's cheerful voice rose above the disturbing sounds. "Good job, Gordon," she exclaimed. I wanted to cry.

I excused myself to go to the restroom where I quickly burst out in tears. *Lord, what can I do here? I thought I could handle this—but it's clear I can't.*

A staff member came into the ladies' room and heard me crying. "If I may be so bold, I think I understand why you're upset. Don't feel bad. If this is your first experience here it's a lot to take in."

"I don't know what's the matter with me," I said. "My brother has cerebral palsy—but his case isn't as severe."

"It's a shock at first seeing what these people have to live with, but you'll get used to it," she said. "I promise. They don't have special guests that often. It means a lot that you've come to visit."

I composed myself and went back into the cafeteria. Most of the folks were finished eating and I noticed a surprising atmosphere of joy.

A young woman wheeled towards me. "Hello," I said, not sure if she was able to speak. "I'm Marji. I've come to sing to you today. Would you like to hear a song about Jesus?"

The most beautiful smile spread across her face. "Oh ... I luh Dee-dus!" she exclaimed. I felt a joy spread across my heart. *Lord, I sense the moving of Your special grace.*

The staff wheeled the people back into the classroom and parked them in a semi-circle around where I was to stand. The minute I got out my guitar, everyone erupted with excitement. It was as if they'd already determined I'd be a blessing. Their hearts were open and receptive. I began to relax and kid with them like I always did with my brother.

"Okay everybody, now that your bellies are all full—NO napping allowed!" The whole group burst out with laughter. "If you fall asleep, I'll have to walk over and give you a big fat kiss to wake you up!"

The men cheered the loudest. We were instant friends. The slightest silliness brought a joyful reaction. They laughed easily, just like my brother.

I sang for about twenty minutes and then shared my testimony. "I didn't grow up learning about God, but one day a friend asked me if I'd like to have Jesus come and live in my heart. I wasn't too sure how that worked, but I wanted Him in my life. The joy and music in my heart comes straight from Him. How many of you would like to ask Jesus to come by His Spirit and live in your heart, too?"

Slowly...one by one, *every* hand was raised the best they could.

Janet's eyes were full of tears as she closed the meeting with a simple prayer. She walked me to the door and gave me a warm hug. "God is so good," she whispered.

"I can't believe how joyful they are despite their challenges. We should never complain about a thing."

Janet closed her eyes and nodded, "That's God's Hand of special grace—just like your babysitter said. I'm sure of it. They are generally very happy, joyful people."

I left knowing God had given me special grace for MY special need to love these people for one reason, and one reason alone: because they breathe.

The next time I visited Janet's class was at Christmas time. After I sang a few songs, Janet announced that Gordon wanted to be the one to put the last candle in the advent wreath. She wheeled him to the front of the room and slowly pulled back his fingers, placing the candle in his hand. Gordon couldn't bend his arm from the shoulder. The only way to get his hand to the advent wreath was by twisting his entire body.

I watched in amazement as Janet slowly moved Gordon's unwieldy body. Her determination to help him be involved brought tears to my eyes. Steadily and carefully, Janet moved Gordon's arm until the tip of the candle slid into the correct hole on the wreath. I watched in amazement. *He's done it.*

As I reached for the matches to light the advent wreath, I noticed a worried expression on Janet's face. Gordon's grip was like steel. He couldn't let go of the candle. Janet glanced up at me and mouthed the words, "please pray."

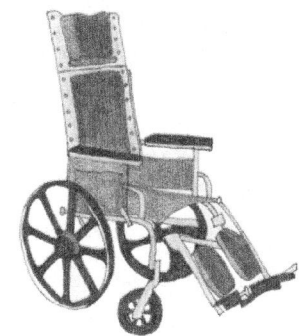

Gordon seemed to understand that he was in danger of breaking, or bending the candle. An expression of pain spread across his face. Gordon was trying with all his might to open his hand. *Lord, please don't let him be embarrassed in front of his friends. Help us.*

"Okay, everybody ... Last time I was here you all asked Jesus to come and live in your hearts, remember? We have a problem. Gordon is *so strong*; he's having trouble opening his hand. Jesus hears our prayers. So, let's ask Jesus to help him."

Everybody bowed their heads as I prayed, "Dear Jesus, please help Gordon relax his hand so we can light the advent wreath. Amen."

Something truly miraculous happened. Gordon's fingers began to move—ever so slowly. One by one, they opened until the candle sat securely, perfectly, right where it needed to be.

In that moment, a miracle happened to me, too. I was enveloped by an overwhelming sense of the unconditional love of God for Gordon. I threw my arms around him, and pressed my cheek against his face. I felt the tension leave Gordon's body. His arms fell to his sides, his body stopped twisting and his chin dropped to his chest as though he was unconscious.

Everyone watched in awe as Gordon sat motionless in his chair. Tears streamed down our faces as we witnessed a sweet move of God upon our dear friend. For almost a half hour Gordan remained completely free of spasms. No one spoke. The atmosphere in the room was thick with the presence of God's Spirit.

There are questions that we won't have answered until we get to heaven. But one thing is for sure—God always provides special grace for our special needs. I've watched it operating in my brother his entire life. Through his multiple surgeries and visits to the hospital, through agonizing physical therapy and heart-wrenching rejection from people who don't understand, George has exhibited incredible courage and joy. As a young adult he developed his own business cutting lawns and making lawn mower repairs. His faith has anchored him through many hardships, and God has developed him into a powerful man of prayer. George is now married to a lovely, disabled woman named Sandra. They live in their own home, and are completely independent.

* "Cerebral palsy is a group of disorders that affect movement and muscle tone. It's caused by damage to the brain, most often occurring before birth. It causes impaired movement associated with exaggerated reflexes, floppiness or spasticity of the limbs and trunk, unusual posture, involuntary movements, unsteady walking, or some combination of these.[1]

[1] Cerebral palsy, https://www.mayoclinic.org/diseases-conditions/cerebral-palsy/symptoms-causes/syc-20353999

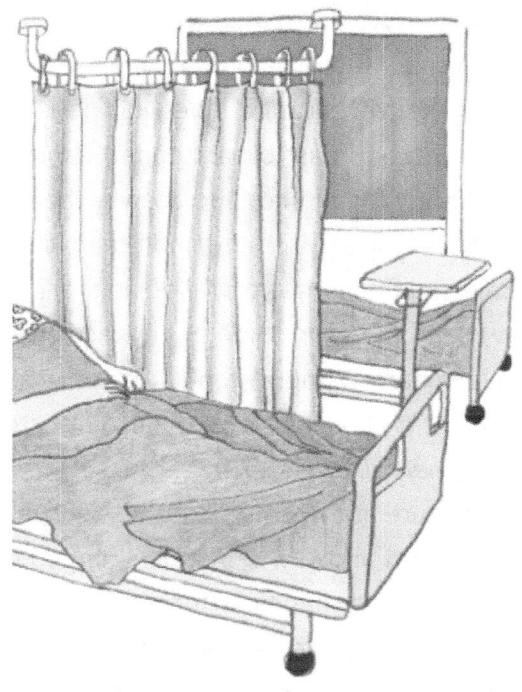

CHAPTER EIGHTEEN

Two North

Upon visiting the county home and meeting Philip, it became clear to me that volunteers serve an important role. The Lord kept nudging me in that direction, so I decided the best place to start was to go and talk to the chaplain. Because there are so many needy patients, he suggested I choose two or three and be faithful to visit them. He asked me a few questions, then decided I should start with Nellie and Francis on Two North.

Two North is a floor for long-term chronic cases. The sights and sounds were overwhelming. *What have I gotten myself into?*

Help me, Lord. Everything in me wanted to turn around and escape to the fresh air that awaited outside.

I had to maneuver around lines of parked wheelchairs, medical equipment, and past the extended hands of the elderly who waited patiently for someone to answer their calls. Haunting voices called out in distress from behind drawn curtains.

"May I help you find what you're looking for?" asked a nurse. She must have read the expression on my face and reassured me that the people I heard crying weren't in pain.

My God! What is this place? My heart wrenched within me. *What am I doing here, Lord?*

I tried not to stare at the unpleasantness around me, but I did glance into one room and saw a person slumped over in a high-backed wheelchair. This shapeless form, silhouetted against the dirty hospital windows, created a picture of hopelessness. I couldn't tell if it was a man or a woman, until I read the name on the door: *MARIE.*

Lord, what happened to this woman? Her head was misshapen and badly swollen with only a few random wisps of hair. Machines pumped out life-giving support. She seemed barely alive. I hesitated briefly, then turned away. *I can't visit this person, Lord, it's too upsetting.*

Nellie

The next room happened to be Nellie's. She was a breath of fresh air. Her room was full of light, decked with cards, flowers, and potpourri. It heralded the attention of a loving family and friends. She wore a pink flannel nighty and big plastic earrings and her nails were beautifully polished. I learned that Nellie had been bedridden for over twenty years. She was totally blind and unable to sit or walk. Instead, she had to be hoisted on a hospital Hoyer lift from bed to chair, to bath, and back again. She lived totally dependent upon the staff for every physical need. Nellie was a Christian and she radiated joy and lightheartedness despite her limitations.

"Hi, Nellie, my name is Marji. The chaplain suggested I visit you today."

She smiled broadly. "Hi, do you have kids? I have ten children, thirty grandchildren and four great grandchildren. I can't see you ... what do you look like?"

Nellie spoke in run-on sentences probably because she was so excited to have a visitor. I tried to answer her questions before she could ask another one. I asked if she'd like to hear a song. She smiled, so I started to sing. However, within moments, she interrupted me. "Where do you live? What does your house look like? What color is your kitchen? Do you have a dog? I used to have a cat? Do you have a cat?"

Apparently, music wasn't what Nellie enjoyed. I put the guitar down, and we spent the rest of our time talking about my farmhouse and her grandchildren. We talked for over an hour and she made me promise to come back. I stepped out of her room

and looked for a nurse to direct me to Francis' room.

Francis

Francis was a frail and tiny woman who lived at the opposite end of the hall from Nellie. Her space was much bigger than the other rooms. It had huge windows that overlooked the property.

The walls of Francis' room were bare. There were no crayoned pictures from grandkids, no flowers, no cards or letters. It appeared as if Francis had no family looking out for her. I later learned Francis believed she had to hide everything or it would be stolen by the staff.

"You have a lovely room here," I said after introducing myself.

"It's cold."

"These big windows are wonderful."

"Too much light—can't sleep."

We weren't off to a very good start. "I brought my guitar, Francis, would you like me to sing to you?"

"No, I want cream puffs from Morgan's Bakery on Clifton Avenue," she insisted. "If you don't know where that is, look it up." Then she turned over in her bed and faced the wall. End of discussion.

Francis seemed desperate for someone to help with the errands she no longer could do for herself. I sympathized with her frustration, picturing her lying in bed yearning for cream puffs that were clearly beyond her reach.

I never learned Francis' prognosis, but I was aware that she lived with constant pain. *Lord, how can I help her?* I didn't dare touch her, though I wanted to lay my hands on her and pray. "Francis, it was nice meeting you today. I'll go now so you can rest, but I promise to visit again real soon ... and hopefully bring those cream puffs."

She whispered a thank you as I tiptoed from the room. *What a sad, sad woman, Lord. Show me how I can bless her.*

Nellie and Francis loved the Lord, but their situations were so very different. Both of them were bedridden, and both had severe physical challenges, but Francis was alone while Nellie had the support of friends and family.

As I headed toward the elevators, I passed Marie's room again. I paused, feeling a slight tug on my heart, but quickly dismissed it. *I can't handle any more sadness today. I've been here long enough.* Besides, I reasoned, the chaplain didn't assign me to Marie.

A welcome gust of cool, fresh air greeted me as I swung open the heavy brass doors of the home. I inhaled a deep, satisfying breath, relieved that I could walk away from the suffocating sadness inside that old building. I shivered, thinking of those eerie gargoyles that sat high on their lofty perches peering down at me as I walked to my car.

The Lord's Way is Perfect

For the next several weeks I visited twice a week and grew accustomed to being on Two North. I found cream puffs for Francis and she seemed to be responding to our visits. Nellie continued her delightful chatter and I had the chance to meet the daughter behind her lovely manicure.

One day, I entered Nellie's room and saw the curtain next to her bed was drawn. "Oh, I see you have a new roommate. That will be nice for you, Nellie."

From behind the curtain, a nurse said, "We'll be done here soon and you can visit." Moments later, she drew back the curtains, and ... there lay Marie.

This was much closer than I ever wanted to be. What had been the Lord's tug on my heart became unavoidable close proximity, but evidently, God was having His way.

"She's in a coma," said Nellie.

"That's right," responded the nurse. "Marie hasn't moved or

said anything in over a year, but I'm sure, in her own way, she would enjoy a song. It's nice that you're visiting."

My hesitancy subsided as I approached her bedside. "Hello, Marie, my name is Marji. I'd like to sing a song for you if that's okay?" Marie was unresponsive.

There but for the grace of God go I ... I began to play my guitar. *Help me get through this without crying, Lord.* A peace settled over me as I looked down at this broken woman, so pale, so motionless. Softly I began to sing: "Jesus loves me, this I know, for the Bible tells me so ..." I wasn't sure Marie even knew I was there. "Little ones to Him belong. They are weak but He is strong ..."

A single, glistening tear formed at the corner of her eye and slowly trickled down her cheek. She moved her hand slightly as if reaching for mine. *Is she responding to me? Or, is this just a muscle twitch?*

"She knows you're there," said Nellie. "Tell her about your kids."

I stayed for only a few more minutes, but I departed with an overwhelming feeling of amazement. I regretted being hesitant to approach Marie. *Lord, forgive me.* I looked forward to seeing her again during my next visit.

When I came back a few days later, I noticed that the curtain in Nellie's room was open and the bed was empty. "Did they move Marie again?" I asked.

"She died!" said Nellie. "Last night."

The same nurse came in and warmly greeted me. "Hello again. Nice to see you."

"I'm so sorry to hear that Marie passed away last night," I said.

"Yes, Marie died peacefully in her sleep around midnight. But did you hear what happened right after you left?"

"No, tell me," I said, tossing my coat over the chair.

"Marie said a word! She spoke for the first time in over a year."

"Oh, my goodness, that's amazing. Did you hear what she said?"

With an almost reverent tone, the nurse replied, "Yes, she said '*JESUS*.'"

A shiver ran up my spine. "Jesus?"

"Yes. She said the name Jesus."

I was stunned. Marie was the third patient I was meant to visit. The chaplain didn't pick her, God did. Despite my delayed reaction to her, God's timing was perfect. Marie couldn't have seen anything with her physical eyes, they were closed. She wasn't looking at *me*. Rather, looking with the eyes of her spirit, she saw Jesus.

My journal entry that day read:

"Two North provided a memorable classroom for me. I learned there's nothing coincidental in the life of a believer. How very important it is to yield to the promptings of the Holy Spirit, even when it's difficult—even when we don't, at first, understand why. I learned more about the Father's love and to what lengths He'll go to show how much He cares about those dear souls on Two North. It's a lesson I'll never forget. We don't know the mysteries that lie in the moments right before death. But I do know that God is not willing that any should perish (2 Peter 3:9).

"I also learned that serving God doesn't have to be complicated—a cup of cold water in His name, a song, a listening ear, a hug, a smiling face. And yes, even going out of your way to buy cream puffs from a certain bakery on Clinton Avenue."

"Religion that is pure and undefiled before God the Father is this: to visit orphans and widows in their affliction, and to keep oneself unstained from the world" (James 1:27 NKJV)

CHAPTER NINETEEN

Fred

I went back to the county home the next week. Francis rolled over when she heard me enter her room. "Oh, good. It's you," she said. "You have to go see my brother, Fred."

"Hi to you too," I chuckled. "Who's Fred?"

"He's my 92-year-old brother."

"I'll be glad to. What floor is he on?"

"He's not here, he's in the hospital. He doesn't know the Lord and I think he's dying. You have to go there and save him."

"Well ... uh ... that sounds like a job for Jesus." I was attempting to lighten things up a bit, but it didn't work.

"He'll listen to you, you're pretty." Francis rolled back on her side, obviously in pain. "He lives in the inner city. He was standing at his kitchen sink last week when two kids burst through the door, attacked him with a hammer, and stole seven dollars."

"That's horrible, I'm so sorry. Is he all right?"

Francis let out a pitiful groan and rolled onto her back. "NO, I told you, I think he's dying. Those kids weren't happy when they found out he only had seven dollars, so they hit him again. Now he's in Mercy Hospital. You have to go."

Mercy Hospital was in a rough neighborhood on the edge of downtown. I didn't like driving in that area alone. I questioned if it was wisdom to go. "Francis, I'll ask my husband, Bill, and see what he says. Maybe he'll go with me in the next few days."

"NO! You have to go TODAY—right away."

Francis was through chatting. She pulled the covers up to her chin and closed her eyes. I said a brief prayer and left. As I walked to my car, I felt agitated. The urgency of her request certainly moved me, but there was no time to drive all the way to the other side of the city and make it home in time for the school bus. "Lord, what should I do?" I sensed Him saying to go the next morning.

Later that evening I discussed it with Bill. He listened for twenty minutes as I laid out all my concerns, then he said, "If God told you to go, then go. Keep in mind, if the guy doesn't want to be saved, there's nothing you can do." Then he added, "I hate hospitals. I'm glad I'm not the one He's sending there."

"Never say 'never.' God has His ways of getting us to do what He wants us to do."

It was a long night. I hardly slept. I went through my usual routine: breakfast, school lunches, waiting for the bus. Once Bill and the boys were gone, I picked up my guitar and set out for the hospital. It wasn't easy to find, but after stopping for instructions (only once), I found it.

The man at the reception desk told me Fred was on the third floor and pointed to the red elevators. The county home was challenging enough, but facing a dying man ...? I didn't know what to expect. *What if he's disfigured? What if he doesn't want a perfect stranger intruding on the last moments of his life?* My stomach knotted as I walked down the hall to Fred's room. *Lord, what if he dies while I'm there?*

The curtain around Fred's bed was closed so I waited in the hallway until a nurse came by. I asked her to ask him if he'd like a visitor. Once she okayed it, I stepped around the curtain and was shocked to see him sitting up in bed.

"Hi, Fred, my name is Marji. Your sister, Francis, sent me."

Fred's eyes lit up. The bandage on the top of his head wrinkled slightly as his face broke into a broad smile. Frank wasn't dying. He was very much alive and *frisky.* He scanned me from head to toe. "Well, hello there, you young thing."

I decided I'd better keep things business-like. "Mr. Smith, Francis asked me to come and sing a song for you and tell you about Jesus."

"Well, if you're the one singing, by all means," he said, smoothing a few wisps of hair remaining on the top of his bald head.

Fred's awareness of my female presence made me wonder if I should have brought a chaperone. "Francis is very concerned about you," I said, opening my guitar case. As I leaned over to retrieve my guitar, I could see out of the corner of my eye Frank watching me bend over. *Naughty old man. Lord, what have You gotten me into this time?*

"The songs I sing are from my devotional life with Jesus." As I began to strum my guitar, the rich tones filled the room. I heard another male voice from behind a curtain on the other side of the room. "Hey, Fred, what did you do to deserve this? Can somebody open my curtain?"

Fred barked back, "Mind your own business. I'm busy here."

I started to sing, but suspected he was only half listening. "Fred, do you know Jesus? Francis is longing for you to accept Him into your heart. Would you like to do that?"

Fred said, "If they look like you in Heaven, I want to go there."

That was good enough for me. The inside flap of my Bible had all the instructions for how to lead someone to Christ. It listed the Scriptures to read and a sample prayer. Then I realized I hadn't brought my Bible. At that moment, I couldn't remember a single Bible verse. *Lord, what do I say?*

A prickly feeling of fear washed over me. I felt embarrassed and saddened that I had come so unprepared. Just then, I heard a man's voice, "Knock-knock, Fred, can I open the curtain? It's Pastor Barker …"

Fred smiled, "Come on in. Wait 'til you see my new girlfriend."

Pastor Barker opened the curtain slightly and peeked in, "Well now, Fred, you've outdone yourself this time, you old coot."

Pastor! Oh, thank you, thank you, Lord. "Hi, I'm Marji. We were just talking about Fred accepting the Lord. Your timing is perfect."

"I guess it is," he said. "I was on my way to Buffalo and the Lord told me to turn around immediately and go see Fred. I wouldn't miss this for the world." He came around the curtain carrying a well-worn Bible in his hand.

"Pastor, why don't you do the honors," I said.

Pastor Barker responded gladly. "We go way back, don't we, Fred?" he said, opening his Bible. The sweetest presence of Jesus surrounded us as he read the Word. "Close your eyes and we'll pray." Fred and I closed our eyes as the pastor led us in the prayer of salvation. "Father, thank you for sending Your only begotten Son, Jesus Christ, to die on the cross for our sins. Thank you for destroying the power of sin and death when you rose from the grave. Thank You that You came to give us new life and a fresh, new start." He put his Bible down and took Fred's hand. "Brother, repeat after me: 'Father, please come into my heart, and be the Lord of my life. Help me to know You, and follow You every day. In Jesus' name, Amen.'"

Fred smiled warmly at me. I could still see that flirtatious twinkle in his eye. I leaned down and gave him a kiss on the cheek. "Fred, your sister is going to be so happy."

Pastor Barker chimed in, "Fred, my man, you still have some good years ahead of you. You're too ornery to die now anyway."

We all laughed. Fred put his arms out for another kiss. Then hugged me without a hint of naughtiness, and whispered ... "Thank you."

My journal entry that evening read:

"I can't wait to tell Francis about her brother accepting Jesus Christ. Thank you, Father, for graciously sending help when I needed it. Help me study to show myself approved so I am always ready to clearly proclaim Your Good News.

CHAPTER TWENTY

Blessings and Brown Paper Bags

Black, burly clouds devoured every inch of blue sky, rapidly obscuring the horizon. Deep, rolling thunder growled ominously in the distance. The temperature dipped as swirling gusts of western wind ushered in the earthy scents of summer rain.

When Bill and I arrived at the location for my engagement, we found a somewhat decrepit crusade tent, pitched directly in the middle of a small, mostly flooded, grocery store parking lot. Water, dumped by the recent cloudburst, rippled in waves over the asphalt. We cautiously hopped and tiptoed around several puddles blocking the tent entrance. Our host pastor greeted us with an immense bundle of fresh hay in his arms.

"Welcome! Can't shake your hands just yet. I'm throwing down some straw to soak up the rainwater so people can get in here. I'm afraid the tent sprung some leaks in that downpour."

The tent looked bedraggled, half in and half out of a gigantic pond. It appeared even smaller than I'd imagined. Rickety wooden chairs teetered on the scattered hay. An enormous, weathered hay wagon, spoke wheels and all, was parked in front of the chairs.

"What's the wagon for?" I asked.

"That's our platform for tonight. You'll stand up there nice and dry when you preach and sing, then come down to pray for the people when you're done. Sorry, it's all we've got, but at least everyone will be able to see you real good. Let's hope plenty of people show up to hold down these chairs," he chuckled.

Their sound system featured gigantic, four-foot speakers with two-foot woofers stacked on top. "They'll be able to hear you with no problem," he added proudly. "Maybe the whole neighborhood!"

I stood behind the hay wagon and observed the people as they arrived. They picked their way across hay mounds and sloshed through puddles. Some came in wheelchairs, while others shuffled along appearing quite infirm. The pastor cranked up the sound system and praise songs echoed throughout the neighborhood.

He yelled over the booming music, "That's sure to bring them in."

Yeah, but everyone in the tent goes home with hearing loss. Little grandmas in the front row stuffed tissues in their ears. I felt like I was in a movie.

The pastor hopped on the wagon platform. His wife turned down the music. It was showtime. He whistled loudly through his teeth to gain everyone's attention. The audience looked up.

This pastor's open, easy-going manner, strong faith, and obvious joy in dealing with people, inspired a reality check. A mystery concerning the walk of faith reveals that often it's not until one feels totally inadequate, absolutely the smallest, and completely unusable, that He uses us in the greatest ways.

"PRAISE THE LORD!" he exulted. "Are you ready for God to move?"

The audience responded with loud applause. "We have a very special treat for you tonight. God has graciously sent this fine, young lady to minister to us. Please give a warm, Hiltonville welcome to …."

I stumbled up the rickety homemade steps braced against the hay wagon--not a very graceful entrance. Maneuvering high heels through the cracks in the wagon floor provided one of several physical challenges that night. The height of the platform gave me the feeling of standing far up on a balcony while trying to connect with people on the ground below.

In spite of all these problems, the music rolled out of me. I felt the Lord's undergirding. Singing became easier as I relaxed and let it happen. However, it's impossible for me to hear the music and remain still. Every tiny movement caused my high heels to fall between the floorboards. One time I actually flailed my arms madly to regain my balance. I resembled a confused mallard trying to flap its way into the air with her web feet stuck in the mud! At one point, I nearly fell off the back end of the wagon and had to lunge forward to recover my balance. The audience misunderstood my frantic actions and apparently feared I'd catapult into their midst because everyone in the front rows ducked simultaneously!

Had anybody bothered to mention I'd be preaching from the highest hay wagon in western New York, I would have worn slacks. I worried about people being able to see up my skirt; so, during the entire performance, I leaned over to lower the hem of my dress. Between leaning over to preserve my modesty and rhythmically stepping about to avoid cracks in the hay wagon floor, I somehow managed to contort my body into a weird shape which gave me cramps in my back. Singing "Rise and Be Healed," I clearly resembled the ideal candidate to be the first person in the prayer line.

The pastor hadn't bothered to tell me until I arrived that he'd advertised the meeting as a "healing crusade." *Oh Lord, help.* Coincidentally, my message was on the healing of the paralytic by the pool of Bethesda. When I finished, the pastor called for anyone who wanted healing to come forward. More than half the people present moved toward the front. The reality of my personal helplessness to minister to these people humbled me. *Lord, it's all up to You.*

Does God Have Muscles?

A small boy, about five years old, squirmed through the crowd of grown-ups to get to the front of the line. An older woman, probably his grandmother, stood beside him. His sad, hazel eyes gazed up at me. "Pray for me, I'm bad." Lowering his head and scuffing the straw with his sneaker, he added, "I'm hyperactive."

His eyes suggested he had tried hard to meet the expectations of those around him, but the chemistry of his little body betrayed him. I could see that he'd absorbed the negative labels given to him. He could not begin to imagine himself any different.

"What's your name?" I asked.

"Jeremy," he sighed.

"That's a great name," I said, bending down to look him in the eyes. "Jeremy, can you make a muscle?"

His face brightened, and enthusiastically he lifted up his little arm, wrinkled his face, took a big breath, and made a muscle for me.

"Wow, look at that," I said, squeezing his upper arm. "Jeremy, do you think God has muscles?" He slowly nodded yes. "Well, He sure does, and I'm going to ask Him right now to *give* you *His* muscles to help you be good. Is that alright with you?" A smile stretched across his freckled face. "But before I do, I want you to know you're not bad, you're *learning*. God wants you to be a successful young man. Let's ask Him to give you the muscles you will need. OK?" Jeremy lowered his head and closed his eyes. I prayed a simple, short prayer. Jeremy threw his arms around my neck and gave me a big squeeze.

Labels can build impenetrable strongholds isolating you from the purposes of God. Jeremy's sweet hug carried the healing of God for me as well. I could identify with that little man, and the sadness that comes with negative labels. *God give me Your muscles, too. Release us both from every lie that exalts itself against the knowledge of God.*

Marjorie

The pastor formally closed the meeting, but people lingered for another hour. I was gathering up my things when I saw a woman waiting off to the side to talk to me. It was Marjorie, a woman who often attends my meetings.

I don't know if Marjorie carries labels from her past, but she's never been able to look me in the eyes. I motioned for her to come close. She bowed nervously, apologizing for taking my time. An unidentified skin disease made her face and hands cracked and disfigured with scaly, red sores. She wore brown polyester slacks that hung on her, and a balling gold cardigan with several holes and missing buttons. Whenever she attended one of my meetings, she'd wait until everyone was gone, then she'd hesitantly approach me. Every time she came, she'd give me a gift. "F-f-f-rom the Lord!" she'd stutter. Her gifts were often photos that she'd taken.

Tonight, however, she seemed slightly more confident. Stiffly holding out her gift, without making eye contact, she managed to stammer, "H-here … Th-this is f-for you." She handed me a damp, crumpled, brown paper lunch bag.

"Thank you, Marjorie. Is this another one of your pictures?"

"No-no. Th-the Lord t-told me to give this to you. Th-th-th-LORD did."

I didn't look in the bag because it was too dark, and I was exhausted. "It's too dark in here. Is it alright if I look at it at home?"

"Y-yes...f-f-from the Lord." she repeated. This time she looked into my eyes. "I p-pray for you. I-it's the Lord." Backing away, while pressing her sore looking hands against her sweater, she repeated the message again, "F-f-from the Lord."

Only a few workers remained to rake up the wet hay. My feet and legs ached. I hurt all over and looked forward to hearing Bill's comments on the meeting. But in the car, my also exhausted husband uttered one, solitary phrase, "Be sure to wash your hands!"

Wasn't there anything good worth commenting on? Did he rate the evening a success? Or, was I kidding myself? His prolonged silence indicated disapproval to me. To make it worse, I remembered earlier that evening, after delivering one of my sermon's stronger lessons, glancing over at my husband hoping to see a smile of approval. Instead, he was slumped on a wooden chair, with both arms folded over his chest, mouth wide open, *sound asleep.*

I could feel myself sliding into discouragement. "Lord, please tell me if I did all right." Preaching is often like sowing seeds into the wind. Even when the seed is the best and strongest, you rarely know where it lands, or if it ever takes root.

We pulled into the garage, and Bill grumbled a reminder to bring all my things in and wash my hands. Taking advantage of my private misgivings, the enemy surfaced once more: "You accomplished *nothing!* Your ministry is *worthless!* You thrive on *vain imaginations!*" The combination of exhaustion and discouragement prevented me from taking authority over his lies, and I could feel myself agreeing with him.

When I passed by the garbage cans on my way into the house, I was tempted to throw Marjorie's gift away without looking at it.

The bag was damp and obviously used. I decided it wasn't anything important. I rarely kept her gifts, but I valued the effort it took for her to overcome her shyness and the love behind the gift, so I didn't throw it away.

Too soon the morning rays of sunshine streamed through my window. My body protested as if I'd been in a marathon. Every muscle ached, and so did my heart. Bill had already gone to work. Usually, we get up together, but I had slept heavily and did not hear him leave.

I sat by the window in my prayer chair. "Lord, why do I feel like saying, 'Pray for me. I'm bad?' Will I ever learn how to really trust You, and not lean on my own strength? Will I ever stop measuring myself? It seems as though I'm either consumed with self-doubt or brimming with pride. There is so much work to be accomplished in me. I only want to please You."

The thought came, "Go get the little brown paper bag."

My conscience cringed because I'd already thought the once-used, crumpled paper bag held nothing of value. But again, I heard, "Go get the little brown paper bag!"

Feeling guilty for my lack of gratitude, I walked to the back room where I'd carelessly dropped the bag on my desk. From the depths of that dirty, crumpled up, once used lunch bag, I found a tiny, plastic-beaded crown about two inches in height.

Totally stunned, I gasped, *"A CROWN FOR ME?"*

Then He said, "Do you realize you almost threw away your crown, because you didn't like the package it came in?"

Time stopped. My thoughts whirled back over the events of my life to examine those who'd crossed my path-angels unaware, visitors with messages of encouragement, weary, infirm souls, outcasts from the rich and beautiful, and wanderers without a place to lay their heads. Did they bring crowns with them? Were they ignored or turned away because they weren't of any reputation, or didn't have the title: "Prophet So-and-So?"

Standing in my laundry room with this little beaded crown in my hand, tears streamed down my face. Suddenly I remembered: Every photograph Marjorie had given me over the years, though always dog-eared and out of focus, pictured an open door!

My journal entry the next day read:

"My father used to say every person we meet has something they can teach us. That's a humble, open-hearted way to live. With that in mind, how carefully we must view the precious souls God puts across our paths. We must never assume our meeting is sheer happenstance — not when we're following the Lord. We might be entertaining angels unawares.

P.S. Many months later, I received word from the grandmother of the little boy who called himself "bad." She simply wrote, "Jeremy is a totally different boy."

CHAPTER TWENTY-ONE

Sparrow Song

It promised to be a historic moment as hundreds of women arrived from all over the United States to gather in the largest ballroom in Washington, D.C. As one of the scheduled singers, I felt especially proud to be included among so many famous people. *Maybe this is a sign of bigger things to come.*

I found myself reflecting on past conversations about the concept of fame. Prior to becoming a follower of Jesus, I had experience doing radio jingles, singing in a rock band, and being part of a folk group named "America's Children." Back then, everything was driven by promotion and marketing. As a Christian minister, I struggled with this dichotomy. There's a tension between having faith in God and letting people know about the ministry He has assigned you. However, as I've gained a deeper understanding of the value that God places on actions done in secret rather than those that seek public attention, I have come to trust in God to open doors for my talents instead of promoting myself. I firmly believe that He will guide me and promote me in the way that He sees fit.

This banquet was the biggest event I'd ever been involved in. It was a far cry from mother-daughter banquets and visits to the county home. Unfortunately, no one told me this was a formal dress event. My dress was a polyester shirt-waist off the sale rack at J.C. Penny's. The only new addition to my outfit was a pair of control-top panty hose. I was mortified when the women paraded in with long gowns, diamonds, and furs.

The preliminaries seemed painfully long. First, refreshments were served in the lobby. Long white linen covered tables were decked with elaborate floral bouquets, China teacups, towers of fresh baked cookies, and heart-shaped tea sandwiches. This was a new experience balancing a plate in one hand, a teacup in the other, while standing straight, holding my stomach in, and maintaining a cheesy smile all at the same time. Not an easy task.

To my horror, while holding the perfect ladylike pose, I felt my control-top panty hose creeping down my legs. When I first felt things shifting, I wasn't too concerned. But all of a sudden, the pantyhose took on a mind of its own. The waistband lunged downward, releasing the roll of fat it was supposed to be controlling—what's a girl to do?

Fortunately, the ladies' restroom had a swing door. I karate-kicked it open, ditched the teacup, stuffed the last cookie in my mouth, and made a beeline for the bathroom stall to make the necessary adjustments.

I emerged from the ladies' room just in time to hear the announcement to take our seats. I looked for a seat in the back (in case it happened again), but the master of ceremonies motioned me to the head table. *Huh? I don't want to sit up there.*

The woman preceding me was that year's Dove Award winner. Her rich voice filled the room as she sang a song of victory. Even before she finished the last stanza, people were on their feet with thunderous applause.

"Ladies, introducing—a housewife from Rush, New York—Marji Stevens!"

I stood and forced my legs to take what seemed like a three-mile walk to the microphone. I could hear my mother's words in my head: "Remember to stand up straight, chest high, stomach in. Walk like a lady not like Sam Huff (former N.Y. Giants line backer). Tuck the fanny under, smile, act confident, and above all, BE NATURAL."

A sudden rush of heat turned my cheeks red as I faced the audience. All eyes were on me, and I imagined them sneering at my ordinary polyester dress. "Why would she wear *that* thing to an event like this?" *Lord, please keep my pantyhose up.* For a brief

moment, people paused their conversations, straining their necks to look at me. I stood by the microphone, took a deep breath, and began to introduce my song. To my horror, the sound man wasn't paying attention. In the middle of my opening remarks, he started the soundtrack tape. *Wait a minute! I'm not ready yet!"* My cue to begin came and went - there was no choice but to start singing.

I'd hardly finished the first few lines when it was as if someone sounded an alarm. Waiters, carrying huge trays, poured out of the kitchen and noisily started clearing the tables. Dishes and silverware rattled and clanked, drowning out the gentle accompaniment to the first verse of my song: *"I can almost hear the angels singing glory to the Lamb..."*

It was awful. People at their tables began talking as if I was completely invisible. Even the women at the head table started talking! The woman who sang before turned her back to me and commanded the attention of everyone at her table. In all my years of singing, even in nightclubs, this had never happened. Being home paring carrots would take top billing over this. *I'll be famous after today as the woman who sang during clean-up. What's her name? The singing housewife who walks like Sam Huff.*

No one listened. No one cared. I kept on singing but I was dying inside. *Lord, why did You bring me all the way down here just to humiliate me in front of five hundred women? Couldn't I have learned what You wanted to teach me in the privacy of my living room?*

A distant thought entered my mind: *Remember the sparrow.* Just the week before, the Lord gave me a delightful vision as I took a walk. I visualized a chubby sparrow perched on a branch in front of an old run-down house in the inner city. The little bird was neither impressed nor depressed about where she was. She simply lifted up her head and sang unto the Lord.

Then the vision changed. The little sparrow clung to a tree branch outside the White House in Washington, D.C. Again, this lovely little creature was neither impressed nor depressed about where she was. She simply lifted up her head and sang her love song unto the Lord.

In this split second of time, without missing a note, that vision lifted my spirit. It was so simple. All I needed to do was remember *why* I sing. Not to gain fame, but simply because there's a song in my heart and the **love of Jesus put it there**. I took the lesson of the sparrow, and simply lifted up my head and sang to my Lord. Everyone else and everything else faded from view.

"Come on in ..." I sang, "the family's waiting, come on in, the table is spread." Courage started rising in my heart. "... and the band of the righteous will be praising Him ..." My voice felt anointed with oil.

The atmosphere of the room shifted. The very air seemed charged with life. As a hint of the magnificent presence of the Lord began to fill the place, all distractions ceased. One by one people stopped talking, turned, and faced the platform.

The Lord commanded their attention. I just sang unto Him, and He did the rest. No applause followed my song. Everyone sat motionless.

Flying home, I sat, pensive, staring out the airplane window. *This is the essence of being orange all-the-way-through, isn't it, Lord? You want everything in my life, whether in thought or deed, to be a simple love song to You.* I was relieved to be going home to my little farmhouse in Rush, New York. Below me the billowing clouds looked solid, as if they were firmly-packed snow mountains one could jump and roll on. Their solidness was, of course, deceiving. Much like the praise of man, these masses of filmy vapors suspended in mid-air are not a firm foundation. And like the opinion of man, they change with every new breath of wind.

My husband met me at the airport. We stopped for dinner and I told him all about the trip. "Sounds like God was proving your stuff," he said. "I'm proud of you. The boys will be happy to have you home."

Catching up after being away kept me busy for a couple of days, but my thoughts were never far from the lesson I learned about the chubby sparrow. Later in the evening, I had some quiet time with the Lord and He gave me a song called, *Run the Race*. My favorite line in the chorus is:

> *Lord, help me run this race of life,*
> *and shine just like Your Son,*
> *Oh, wreath of joy, My Savior's voice,*
> *To hear Him say: 'Well done!'*

My journal entry for that day read:

"Becoming a woman of all-the-way-through excellence often includes the unexpected, humbling, and sometimes painful situations that try our faith. Help me keep a song of praise in my heart and trust Your plan no matter what I'm doing."

CHAPTER TWENTY-TWO

Belt Loops and Quad-Runners

Bill planned to go to the gun club one afternoon to compete in a sporting event. There wasn't much for me to do, so I decided to go to the mall and shop. Thankfully, before leaving the driveway, I thought to look in my purse and discovered I'd forgotten my checkbook. Bouncing back into the house I searched for my checkbook, but it was nowhere to be found.

My stomach churned. *Where is that checkbook?* We had just deposited a chunk of money into the account to pay for our son's wedding expenses, plus my Visa card and driver's license were tucked inside the checkbook. *O God, please help me find it.* The picture on my driver's license was so horrible that anyone doing an imitation of a blowfish could pass for me.

My mind whirled. I tore through every one of my purses. *OK, Marj, get a grip. THINK!* A frantic examination of closets, pockets, underneath couches, and beds produced no checkbook.

Be CALM...PRAY! But there was no time for that! I had to find my checkbook. A thought flashed into my mind. *It's at CHURCH!* Ironically, the sermon that morning was entitled, "Misplacing God's Truth."

By the time the pastor concluded his remarks, tears flowed down my cheeks. *TISSUES! That's it.* I remembered taking my checkbook out of my purse to find a tissue. *I must have left the checkbook on the chair.*

I dashed to my car and headed back to the church. It

occurred to me that a rather unkempt visitor sat right behind me during services. *Aha! He took the checkbook and is probably on his way to Bermuda by now.*

Thoughts ricocheted in my mind: checkbook, Visa,

blowfish, Bermuda. Suddenly, I spotted Pastor Mike leaving the church parking lot. Slamming on my brakes, I reversed the car and yelled, "Pastor Mike! Did you find a checkbook?"

"Don't think so, but you can call the church on …" I can't tell you what he said next, because I was already sprinting to the front door of the church. I raced into the sanctuary and began frantically searching all  around and under chairs. NO checkbook!

I lunged at the hapless, head usher who was locking up, and stuck my sweaty red face into his: "DID YOU FIND A CHECKBOOK?" All the while my thoughts echoed: *checkbook, Visa, blowfish, Bermuda.* Somewhat unnerved, the usher shook his head 'no.' I can't tell you what he said next, because his words trailed off into the distance as I ran out the door.

Control yourself, woman … b-r-e-a-t-h-e … but there was no time for that … *checkbook … checkbook … checkbook.*

Bill has it at the gun club. With renewed energy, I sped in the direction of the gun club and decided to take a shortcut. The problem was, I didn't *know a* shortcut. This was hardly the time to invent one. Getting lost was the last thing I needed to do.

Finally, the terrain began to look familiar. *Ahh, at last… relax, Marji. Breathe!* I barreled onto the gun club grounds doing 50 MPH along the dirt driveway, until I saw a man with a shotgun. Gigantic ribbons of dust billowed around me as I slammed on my brakes. "Can you tell me where the sporting clay tournament is happening?" He cupped his hands over his nose and mouth and pointed, "About a mile that way..." I can't tell you what he said next, because I launched down the dirt road full speed again.

CHECKBOOK, CHECKBOOK ... potholes, rocks, nothing slowed me down. I skidded into the sporting clay parking area. When the dust cleared, I realized I was in the center of a gigantic testosterone convention. There wasn't one woman in sight. Nevertheless, I emerged from the center of my dust cloud, hands on hips, feet firmly planted, woman on a mission—*checkbook, checkbook, checkbook*. Scanning the crowd for someone in charge, I spotted a man with a walkie-talkie. "Excuse me. Are you the walkie-talkie man?" The man looked bewildered. "I need to reach my husband. It isn't really an emergency, but it's very important." He shrugged. "I can page him for you."

"No, no," I said. "That would disrupt the tournament and he wouldn't like that. Can't I walk out there to find him?"

"I wouldn't advise it, lady. They're shooting." He removed his camouflage baseball cap and scratched the top of his head. He looked around, adjusted his hat and said, "Got a Quad-runner over here. I can drive you out there to find 'em." My jaw dropped at the thought of me on the back of a four-wheeler with a strange man, but these were desperate times. I tried to explain: "I lost the checkbook and my Visa—driver's license—uh—blowfish—Bermuda..." He nodded in agreement as if to ward off further explanation and motioned me to follow.

He spit a wad of tobacco juice on the ground. "You'll have to hold on tight and grip me with your knees."

What? No way. I can't grip and press. I'm a Christian! "Can't I ride side-saddle?"

"Afraid not, Lady," he shouted as the engine kicked in.

I examined the big, wide, fenders covering the wheels. How could I manage to swing my legs over the back end of that thing? My legs are the same length as my arms. *I'll never be able to make it over! What if I land on the fender and, oh no …*

Suddenly a dreaded memory from kindergarten flooded my mind. All the kids were sitting on the floor when the teacher told us to come closer to her. Without any prior experience to warn me of the sound chubby, bare legs produce when scooting on linoleum, I enthusiastically slid forward. Without  warning, a loud sound squeaked out from under me. The entire class fell silent. One girl pointed her finger, "She Scooched!" I was mortified and vowed I'd never scooch again.

Today, however, was no time to give into the fear of the dreaded scooch. Taking a big breath, I swung my right leg back and forth until I gained good momentum, then flung myself into the air. Miraculously, I landed square on the seat. When the poor guy finally stopped rebounding from the force of my landing, he yelled, "Hold on!"

Fumbling nervously, I stuck my fingers through the belt loops on his pants (tea cup style), being careful not to touch his body. Roaring off into the woods with a strange man, I felt the awkward necessity to say something, anything, just to ease the tension. "Well, this sure beats grocery shopping!"

Holding onto the belt loops of his pants was working just fine, until we hit a bump. When I saw my feet go past his ears, I decided it was time to grip and press.

"Hey lady, does anybody out here look familiar to you?" he yelled.

"Not yet," I bellowed. "I guess I'll have to pick a good one!"

We'd almost covered the entire course. "THERE HE IS!" I shrieked. Bill turned briefly to see me make my grand entrance. He didn't say a word. He calmly turned around and continued the job of scorekeeper. (Maybe he hoped no one would connect him to the crazy lady thundering down the path on a Quad-runner.)

"NOBODY DIED!" I screeched, while dismounting. I bounded up beside him, "Do you have the checkbook?"

After an unusually long pause, even for Bill, he said, "No."

Instantly, tears erupted and I blurted out my dilemma. "I've searched everywhere … the wedding money, and my Visa's in there, and …"

Without one flinch of emotion, without losing one drop of his cool, he said, "You'll find it." End of discussion.

That's it? Not one word of concern? How about nice to see you, honey? It seemed pointless to say any more, so I remounted the Quad-runner, gripped and pressed, and off we flew.

Lord, please, please, help me find my checkbook. Twenty minutes later I edged into our driveway and went inside. There, on my desk, was my checkbook!

I stood wide-eyed. *How could that be? I searched everywhere."* Suddenly the answer came to me. I'd searched all right, but with my sunglasses on. The grain of the checkbook cover blended perfectly with the wood grain of my desktop. Even more humbling, I remembered that before racing down the driveway, a small still voice prompted me, "Why don't you go into the house and check one more time?" My answer had been, "I haven't got time for that!"

Bill came home from the tournament. I heard the door slam, and he asked. "Did you find it?"

"Yup," I answered.

"Where was it?"

"It's a long story..."

My journal entry that day occupied several pages starting with this opening line:

"It's amazing what loops you'll grab when you're believing a lie."

TWENTY-THREE

Bill's Bird Buddies

Whenever I need to simplify and regain my grasp on eternal things, I'm drawn to our living room window to watch the birds. I turn my big, overstuffed chair, push it into position, open the window to let in fresh air, then sit and listen to the birds sing.

Sitting in my chair by the window became especially pleasant when Bill purchased a bird feeder and put it right where I could see it. Watching the birds was so enjoyable that he soon put up several more. Early each morning Bill walked around the yard refilling the feeding stations. "Nothing but the best for my bird buddies," he'd say. The birds became so accustomed to this practice that they'd perch along the fence waiting for fresh manna from their benevolent provider.

This new hobby proved such a success, that Bill decided to expand his operation. He bought feeders for nearly every window. We put suction-cup feeders on the windows. We hung hummingbird feeders along the porch. He even kept a birdie guest book to log the varieties that visited: wren, chickadees, goldfinch, sparrow, nuthatches, blue jays, cowbirds, cardinals, and bluebirds, to name a few.

The bird feeders' ability to attract a crowd surpassed our expectations. As the bird population increased, our sleeping decreased. Early in the morning, while we were still peacefully glued to our pillows, we'd hear their sleepy chirps heralding the rising sun. This cued the morning glee club. It was soothing at first, but that didn't last. Their drifting, lazy sounds soon swelled with great crescendo until the noise became shrill blasts of every conceivable chirp and whistle.

One morning, a tone-deaf bird joined the buddies' choir. It's cheery *da-da-da* ended with a flat *duh-duh* that rattled my musical ear. It was impossible to sleep listening to that *da-da-da-DUH-DUH.*

"BILL, do you hear that? You know, people really can develop serious psychological problems when experiencing sleep deprivation!"

The covers rolled a bit. "So, SLEEP!" he mumbled.

"Impossible!" I sighed and slammed both arms down on the bed. "There's no chance to sleep. BIRDS, BIRDS! That's all I hear."

Bill said nothing. I continued, "Your bird-buddy experiment is getting out of control. Doesn't it concern you that so many new ones arrive each day? It's like being in an Alfred Hitchcock thriller. It's an invasion! I feel like we should board up our windows or something."

Unwilling to address my hysteria at 5:00 AM, birdman Bill slept on. When the alarm went off, he sprang (annoyingly) from bed, refreshed and (disgustingly) filled with enthusiasm to start the day. "Gotta feed my bird buddies!" he chirped.

To my chagrin, Bill drove past a yard one day where homemade, gallon-sized milk jug feeders swayed from every tree limb. Fresh inspiration! Bill started collecting milk bottles wherever he could find them. He cut a little square window about four inches from the bottom on each side, filled it with seed, then tied a rope to the handle. Soon, we had dangling milk jugs swinging from every tree branch in our yard.

Keeping all these feeders filled was expensive. We learned that the Clover Street Farm Market sold a powdery corn mixture they advertised as *"cheap"* and delicious. Bill bought a hundred pounds. I think it was birdie junk food. Bill threatened to print T-shirts with "Big Bill's Birdie King" printed on the front. I was ready to move back home with my mother.

This expanded bounty of feed scored big with the birds—and the entire critter population. Soon, we had squirrels rocketing from feeder to feeder. Our yard became a drive-through for chipmunks, crows, geese, and deer. Then, the biggest visitor arrived – a black bear! We discovered one of the rod iron poles bent in half and the feeder halfway across the neighbor's yard— empty. To confirm our suspicions, we learned a neighbor had all his bee-hives destroyed.

The bear was the last straw. Reluctantly, Bill assessed that his bird buddy hobby had gotten out of hand. Besides, scrubbing bird droppings from porch railings, steps, sidewalks, windows and doors was getting really old. He decided the only wise thing to do was decrease the number of feeders until all that remained were the original few. Perhaps it was too much off a good thing and stole the simple delight that had first inspired him.

The intrusion of that black bear reminded me how the enemy of our souls never misses an opportunity to kill, steal and destroy (John 10:10). I never imagined something as noble as feeding the birds could turn harmful, but even good things can be taken too far. It was fun while it lasted, but fewer feeders would afford Bill and I more special time to sit together to watch the birds like we used to. I was happy that I wouldn't have to weed rogue birdseed plants sprouting in my garden.

We could now afford to replace the cheap bird food with more nutritious wild black seed. Usually, the minute Bill filled the feeders, dozens of birds arrived. But strangely, not a single one approached that day. Something was different, and there was revolt in the treetops. A few brave birds fluttered near, but not one landed to nibble. They wanted their fast-food.

Bill was worried, "It's so good for them. Why don't they at least try it?"

"Where have I heard that line before?" I retorted. "That's the reaction I got when I introduced Tofu and whole wheat spaghetti to the family. You guys 'flew' over the dinner table without stopping to eat." Bill didn't comment.

The next morning, I went to my chair by the window to watch the birds and have a quiet time with the Lord. I was reminded of Jesus' admonition to the Ephesian church in the book of

Revelation: "...I have this against you, you have *forsaken* the love you had at first..." (from Rev. 2:2-4). The words gripped my heart. *Lord, don't let that happen to me.*

At this time, I was receiving invitations to sing and speak several times a month. There were more letters to write, travel arrangements to be made, and records to keep. Often my study and prayers centered only around preparations for the next ministry engagement. Focusing on all the details related to ministering to others, it's easy to miss what God wants to say to me personally. It was like tending to all those feeders that swallowed up the moments Bill and I had to watch the birds together. Some of our sweetest, most intimate conversations happen when there is nothing on our agenda but being together.

The word *forsaken* comes from the Greek verb *egkataleipo*. It means to *leave behind, abandon, desert.* God promises to never leave us, or forsake us (from Hebrews 13:5). *We* are the ones that move away. Tears caught in my throat. *Hold me close, Lord. Don't let me drift away.*

Remembering the feeders, I glanced up to see if any birds had dared to eat the new seed. One fat sparrow perched on the feeder's edge examining the seed. Since it didn't resemble the norm, the bird was cautious. Finally, it took one bite. I think it was the signal the other birds needed. I heard in my heart: *You first must feed yourself, then you will have nutritious life-giving seeds to share.* It's amazing how God can teach us about excellence using something as ordinary as birdhouses made from milk jugs!

Bill called midday to check up on the birds. "Well, did they eat yet?"

"They sure did! It's almost all gone."

"Great. I knew they'd like it as soon as they got up the courage to trust. Gotta go …" Little did Bill know, his brief remark put the finishing touches on the lesson.

My journal entry that day was a little poem:

"The sweetest lessons life can bring,
Are those that teach my heart to sing.
With Christ, each trial and circumstance
Instructs my spirit how to dance.
It's all in how you view a thing:
Is March still winter, or almost spring?
Sometimes, the things most hard for me,
Are God-sent opportunities.
For He is good, and He can see
What makes me grow effectively.

CHAPTER TWENTY-FOUR

Specialness In Commonness

Light, puffy clouds moved gently across the sky. It was a perfect morning to be outside. I drove to my favorite park to take a walk. On my way, the phrase *specialness in commonness* came to mind. It seemed the Lord wanted me to learn some lessons from the ordinary things I observed along the way.

As I approached a small bridge, I heard the sound of rushing water. Curious, I looked over one side of the bridge and saw a picturesque waterfall winding down a steep hillside. *Wow, Lord, this is so beautiful.* Water gleamed with a silvery sheen as it danced over a cascade of craggy rocks. *This is special, but hardly common,* I thought. After a few minutes, I turned to continue my walk when a thought crossed my mind, "Take a look downstream."

I stopped and walked across to the other side of the bridge that led away from the splendor of the waterfall. *There's nothing to see here.* Once again, I turned to leave.

"Let me show you…" He whispered.

Tangled brush and scrubby trees that drooped over the surface made it difficult to see the water. I had to adjust my position and look past all the things obstructing my view of the deep water pooling quietly beneath the bridge. I paused, hoping to see what the Lord wanted to show me.

My thoughts drifted back to my visits at the county home. I remembered how difficult it was to go there at first. These weren't 'waterfall' people. They didn't attract visitors. On the contrary, they often repelled them. Disabled, poor and forgotten, their beauty was easily missed.

I also remembered the sweet lady I'd met at a Bible Study. Her name was Debbie. I'd never seen Debbie at the study before, but I felt strangely drawn to her. She seemed painfully shy and rather care-worn. After the study, there was time allocated for refreshments and fellowship. Most of the women were old friends so their conversation flowed freely. As the women talked and laughed, I noticed Debbie wasn't joining in. She stood on the outside of the circle, obviously uncomfortable. A few times she tried to say something, but immediately got cut off. Debbie would retreat back into the shadows, and the saddest expression clouded her face. This happened several times until I'd had enough.

"Excuse me! Debbie, it's nice that you joined us today. Did you want to share something?" I asked. Everyone stopped talking and glanced toward Debbie, who at that point, seemed a bit unsure what was happening. She stuttered awkwardly and finally got out a few words. The group's attention quickly turned away. I realized I'd put her on the spot, so I pulled her aside to apologize.

Talking one on one seemed painful for her. I found out she lived two miles from my house. That's when I heard the Lord say, "I want you to be her friend." I knew it was no accident I'd met her, but I didn't know how to bridge the shyness.

Later that week, the Lord nudged me to call Debbie before leaving for the grocery store. I felt a little awkward since I didn't know her, but I called. She answered the phone and I learned she had no means of transportation. "Do you need to go to the grocery store," I asked. "I'm going in a little while. Can I pick you up?" She seemed delighted.

When I stepped inside Debbie's house, I noticed an unfamiliar smell. "What'cha cooking'?"

She hesitated a moment. "Pinto beans."

"I've never tried cooking those. Do you make them often?" I asked.

Debbie didn't reply, but later I learned that beans were the family's primary food source. Before long, a weekly routine developed and Tuesdays became our day to bargain hunt. We visited the regional farm market, and the bread outlet store, then the grocery store. I always had multiple bags of groceries compared to her one or two, even though her family was twice the size of mine. Some weeks she bought nothing. By accident, one time, her purse opened and I observed it was totally empty—not a comb, a wallet, money—nothing.

Debbie's family was poor. I had not confronted such poverty before, which put me in a dilemma. I could rush in and buy groceries for her, assuming I was being a good Christian by doing so, but it seemed to me Debbie was a proud, and very private woman who might interpret my good intentions the wrong way. *Lord, show me how I be a good friend to Debbie.*

I looked forward to shopping each week with Debbie, and she gradually became more comfortable with me. Debbie shared about growing up in the mountains of West Virginia in a tiny home with no electricity or indoor plumbing. She talked about the few times she was allowed to go to church and how she loved to hear about Jesus. Debbie didn't talk about her health, but terrible sores on her skin exposed health issues.

I wanted to give Debbie a gift, beyond anything in the natural. I wanted to be a friend who listened, but Debbie turned the tables and became a listening ear for me. As I shared my life struggles, she often encouraged me with, "Don't worry, the Lord will help you through." Though Debbie had so many challenges in her own life, she never complained or exhibited an ounce of self-pity. Debbie was a victor not a victim.

The farm market sold vegetables in quantities too large for my family. One day, I was looking to buy broccoli, but they were only selling it in a large basket. "Hey Debbie, this is too much broccoli for my family. It'll spoil before we can eat it all. Does your family like broccoli?" She received it gladly knowing she was helping me out.

When I dropped Debbie off each week, she would wave good-bye with abundant "thank-yous" as if I had performed some amazing feat. I believe the greater blessing was mine.

A cool, fall breeze blew against my face. I shuddered and drew my collar up against my cheeks. Tossing a flat pebble over the side of the bridge, I picked up a steady pace and started toward home.

If the Lord had not impressed me to befriend Debbie, I might have missed the wonderful blessing of knowing her. Like the deep pool obscured by twigs and branches, I needed to adjust my perspective and find an opening to see the beauty glistening underneath. Debbie fit the description of a "downstream" person, but out of her quiet, Christ-centered heart, flowed true riches.

That evening I read a verse in Proverbs (24:32) which speaks of a man who learns an important lesson while passing the overgrown, neglected field of a slothful man. When he saw the field, he "considered it well...and received instruction." The man gained wisdom observing the parables nestled along an ordinary walk. That overgrown field turned out to be a life lesson for all of us.

I wrote in my journal that day:

"We'll find *specialness in commonness* whenever we take the time to see people, and the world around us through God's eyes—like hidden pools in streams on a country path."

PS. The cause of Debbie's poor health was later discovered, she received the medication she needed and her whole life changed. Our shopping adventures became sporadic as my ministry grew and Debbie got her own transportation. Now she was free to go whenever and wherever she wanted. And Debbie started traveling. In fact, she became a world traveler. Debbie's transformation was remarkable—a testimony of God's faithfulness and her strong belief that, "God will help you through."

CHAPTER TWENTY-FIVE

Test of a Good Pilgrim

I hate clutter. To fight it, I'm always trying to downsize the overabundance of 'stuff' that creeps in to our home. At one point, I was the care-keeper of all my mother's, my mother-in-law's, and my grandmother's things. Our farmhouse came completely furnished. We had antique tools, new tools, fishing rods, shot guns, trapping equipment, and skis. We added drum sets, conga drums, bongos, keyboards, several guitars, and a giant sound system. Plus, all my art supplies, sewing stuff, and cook books. What's a clutter-hater to do?

With so much stuff, we needed lots of plastic totes to store it in. Bill had his totes and the boys had their totes. We even had a tote for the dog! Being a dyed-in-the-wool clutter hater, I couldn't escape feeling frustrated, overwhelmed and somewhat guilty.

At one point in my son's adolescence, I discovered he was collecting apple cores in a can under his bed so he could add up how many apples he ate in a month! Consequently, we also started collecting mice!

The Bible calls believers "pilgrims and sojourners" (2 Peter 2:11). The test of our possessions should be whether or not it travels well. Jesus doesn't tell us *not* to accumulate, He tells us *where* to accumulate; not to lay up treasures on earth, but to lay up treasures in heaven. (Matthew 6:19).

The greatest lesson about material possessions came to me on my visit to Africa in 1985. I was invited to be the soloist on a mission trip to Uganda, Zaire, and Kenya. We were planning to be gone for three weeks. Not knowing what to expect, I was advised to bring as much as I thought I'd need. After multiple trips to the mall, I finally had everything. On the day of departure, I tightened the straps on my suitcase and surrendered it to the airlines. Somewhere between Kenya and Uganda my suitcase got lost.

"The airlines will find it and bring it to where I'm staying--right?" The official at the airport said, "No problem" (which was the common answer I got for almost every question). He started opening up his desk drawers to find the "official report paper," but I observed the drawers were all empty! I later learned you don't usually get lost luggage back. If it turns up, it's destroyed and all the contents stolen.

When I saw there was no official paper, I knew I was in trouble. "You'll find it for me, won't you?" I asked, choking back the tears. At that point, the missionary tactfully steered me away before I "cross-examined" the man further and whispered, "We'll have to pray."

All I had to wear was the old blue dress and cheap plastic beads I'd traveled in. The dress was *dry-cleaned only!* With one stroke of human error, I was reduced to total *"stufflessness."* During the next week, the weather was hot and sticky. I dared not wash the dress out of fear that it might shrink and I'd have to spend the entire time hiding in my bedroom. I also had no combs to hold back my wild, recently permed hair, no deodorant, no make-up ... nothing! All my precious stuff had vanished into the black hole of lost airline luggage.

It was a shock to realize how attached I was to my things. I even had withdrawal symptoms from having no variety and choice. The Lord gave me grace not to complain (too much), but it was a struggle. Having my things gave me a sense of security so far from home. There weren't any malls in this part of Africa. Nor could I run to a drug store for deodorant.

Eventually, when I stopped struggling and listened, the Lord gave me a fresh perspective. It became clear that He had arranged this for a purpose. Once I settled into that thought, I began to anticipate what He was going to do. Remarkably, I felt unencumbered and free. Life became simple, with my God-appointed uniform, the old, blue dress.

Our purpose in visiting Uganda was to conduct a women's leadership conference. Women came from miles away. Many walked for days, often carrying their babies on their backs, along with a simple sack of supplies to last the *entire* week.

We were greeted with the cheers of dozens of children as our old Volkswagen Beetle bumped down the rough, red clay roadway. The missionary I was traveling with had played my music for the church on her previous visit, and promised she'd bring me to visit and sing.

"Lady in the box!" They cheered. "Lady in the box!" I was greeted with enthusiastic hugs and handshakes. Little fingers poked curiously through my kinky new perm and in and out of my open-toed shoes.  One little lad, fascinated by the feel of my stockings, kept running his hand up my leg. Another little fellow snapped my nylons and looked up at me in amazement as if to say, "What kind of skin is this?" I diverted his attention away from my nylons by slipping off my white beads to let him try them on. That initiated a huddle of little ones who also wanted to try on the beads from America. I sensed the cultural walls melting away as each child approached. God's love grew inside me.

The next day, we gathered at the church for the women's conference. The sight of their African dresses against the deep green jungle was breathtaking. The women moved gracefully like multi-colored walking bouquets. Each morning as the breakfast fires curled smoke into the air, the women spread their dresses out across the lawn in the sun. The surrounding field transformed into a shimmering patchwork of rainbow colors. Watching the women waiting beside their dresses in their undergarments let me know we had something very special in common—we each had only one dress.

The loss of my suitcase suddenly took on a whole new meaning. It occurred to me that my dress was an assignment from the Lord. This insight came from a book I'd read by Norman Grubb called, *Reese Howells: Intercessor.* Rees Howells worked as a coal miner in Wales in the late 1800's. He lived the life of a miner in order to pray for the men working there. He learned to pray with miraculous results as he walked out the challenging disciplines God gave him. Mr. Howells inspired millions of people with his remarkable life of prayer. "The path of the intercessor is the way of the cross." After years of powerful ministry, he founded a Bible College in Britain, to teach the principles of faith and intercession that God had given him. The ministry of Rees Howell, and his son, Samuel Howells, greatly impacted the history of the twentieth century.

Later in the week, I was invited to sing at the Uganda National Theater. A Ugandan brother, named David Polopollo, studied music in the United States from approximately 1981-1985. During his stay in the states, someone gave him a cassette of my music. Now back in his own country, David prepared a two-hour concert to be presented at the National Theater. Somehow, he learned that I was in the country and contacted the missionary home where I was staying. Although David had been preparing for years to share his music with the people of his nation, he graciously offered to give me one whole hour of his time. Normally, such an event would require lots of preparation. I'd probably shop for a new dress, get my hair done, fuss over my nails, (and try to lose a little weight). But there was no time for that. I only had one hour to get to the theater. I smoothed the wrinkles on my blue dress, adjusted my white beads, and went.

The auditorium seated over a thousand people. It was filled to capacity. I watched from backstage as people filed in. David and his choir were to perform for the first hour. It was a stunning sight to see forty white-robbed men and women standing against burgundy drapes. David sat at the grand piano. The auditorium grew silent until David gave the awaited nod. Their voices sent goosebumps up and down my arms.

The choir finished the last song and David introduced me. I felt so small walking out on that giant stage all by myself. *Lord, please enable me.* All my songs were in English, but the Lord had assured me He wouldn't let language be a barrier. Halfway through the first song I felt His anointing. I focused on one point near the ceiling and imagined the Lord sitting there. I sang like I'd never sung before. Heads bowed, tears glistened, and hands raised all over the room. When my performance was over the audience erupted with applause. It was reported that many gave their heart to the Lord, and some experienced physical healing. All I did was worship Him, and He did the rest.

Miraculously, my suitcase arrived on the day we were to depart. I sat on the floor of my room and opened the suitcase filled with new clothes. But I didn't have peace. The choices overwhelmed me and I felt convicted looking at the excess. I had the distinct sense that I was NOT to change my clothes. Doing that would spoil something far more important than fresh attire. So, I pulled the well-worn blue, stinky dress off the bed and slipped it on.

As I walked into the church, three ladies rushed toward me and ushered me into another room and began to remove my dress. Then they pulled out a brand new, hand-made, green and white dress and slipped it over my head. It fit me perfectly! They tied the sash snugly around my waist, tugging here and there, then stepped back and smiled. They escorted me back into the sanctuary while a hundred and fifty women burst into cheers. Soon everyone was dancing, including me. It became evident that throughout the week, the women were secretly measuring me with the span of their hands each time we hugged. One sweet woman came up afterwards and said, "I've been watching you with one dress all week. You have taught me patience."

The miraculous events of that trip left a profound impact upon my life. Returning to America, I was determined to make downsizing a priority. I actually experienced a little culture shock. Excess was everywhere. My first visit to the supermarket left me immobilized in the doorway. Surveying the extravagance of every conceivable food, flavor and variety imaginable, I felt ashamed. All I could think of were those beautiful women gratefully scooping their meals with their fingers from simple bowls in outdoor kitchens. I thought about the babies I saw sleeping in wheelbarrow beds, and mothers stretching their arms toward heaven to drink from the Lord while their babies drank milk from their bare breasts. Memories of their songs and smiles made it hard for me to step back into my world as if nothing had happened.

The somber warnings from James flooded my mind and became my journal entry for the day:

"The rusting of our treasures will be a witness against us (from James 5:3). For where my treasure is, there will my heart be (from Matthew 6:21). The danger is not in the treasure itself; the danger is in the heart investment that treasure demands. The test of a good pilgrim is to know what travels well; to keep a light grip on the things of this world, and make our life's investment count for eternity. What we hold onto in this life, we'll lose. What we risk to give away in Jesus' name – we'll keep forever. Amen.

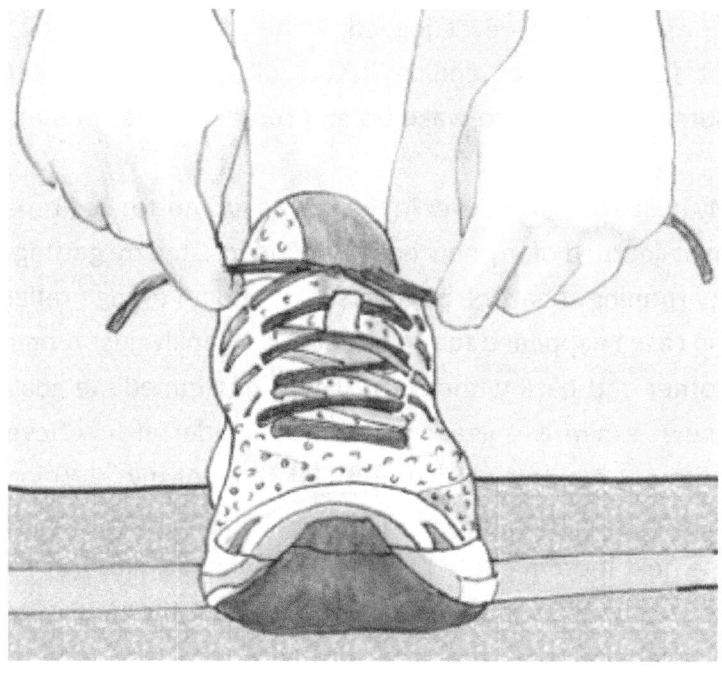

CHAPTER TWENTY-SIX

The Impossible Mile

Occasionally I experience a glorious season of self-discipline when I possess the needed willpower to exercise and eat healthy. These times are usually short lived, and each time I fantasize that they will last forever.

Anything even approaching consistent self-discipline has eluded me over the years. My internal wrestling in this arena plays out often in my prayers and on the pages of my journal. Though it has always been my desire to stay on the path of a healthy lifestyle, an unexpected thought dropped into my mind one day.

Jog. Jog? Me?! I've never jogged. None of my friends jog, and except for my never ending battle with the bulge, there is absolutely no reason to wake up and run down the road at 5:00 A.M.

My husband is a believer in the Boy Scout motto: Be Prepared. When he learned of my new endeavor, he insisted on getting high quality running sneakers, padded socks, and an orange reflective vest, in case I happened to run after dark. (Frankly, just running to the corner and back without dying was my immediate goal.) All this new expensive gear made me wonder if my level of commitment would ever live up to the cost of my $120 jogging shoes.

The next morning at 5:00 A.M. I was wide awake. This hadn't happened since my kids were little. Clutching the new gear laid out the night before, I crept from my bedroom. *What's gotten into me? Who knows, maybe I'll discover some latent Olympic ability buried deep within me all these years.*

The morning air was crisp and sweet with the scent of honeysuckle. Mist curled lazily across the valley. A solitary morning dove perched on the telephone wire cooing out its song. It was the perfect morning to begin my new career as a runner. I confidently headed down the road. "This is great!" I exclaimed to the birds. "I must be born to run!"

In my mind, the goal was clear. Run to the corner. However, before the corner was anywhere in sight, every cell and muscle in my body screamed in protest. Gasping, I limped to the side of the road. *This can't be good for me,* I thought, bending over, gulping for air. *I hope the neighbors aren't awake. This is too embarrassing for an audience. Maybe this just isn't my gift.* Then I remembered my $120 sneakers.

The next morning, to my amazement, I awoke again at exactly 5:00 AM. The same strange motivation propelled me out the door. A little progress was becoming visible, but the goal of running the four-mile block loomed very far in the distance. The third day dawned gray and drizzling. I rolled over in bed and pulled the covers over my head. *I think I'll take the day off.* But there was no way to ignore the inner promptings. *NO. Get up! You've got to do this!* My enthusiasm remained stuck on empty, but I pried myself out of bed.

Bill staggered into the kitchen behind me, "You're not going out in this, are you?"

"Don't tempt me," I groaned, slipping on my rain poncho.

"Better you than me," he mumbled, shaking his head.

To my surprise, running in the rain was invigorating, but soon pains and breathlessness began to slow me down.

I was on the verge of discouragement when a thought suddenly entered my mind: ***Lean in! You have need of endurance.***

It didn't make any sense to me, but I obeyed that thought and literally leaned as far forward as possible without falling over. That's when it happened ...

I'd heard about a phenomenon called the "second wind." It's a sudden burst of energy known as a runner's high, when the brain's "feel-good" neurotransmitters are released. I knew God was *firing me up* to prevent me from *giving up*.

To my amazement, new strength trickled into my muscles. Sweat beaded on my brow and across my shoulders. My breathing leveled out and became steady and rhythmic. I ran all the way to the corner and back.

My husband was standing at the end of the sidewalk in his

bathrobe, coffee mug in hand, with a big grin on his face. "GO, Marji, GO!"

I trotted up the driveway, swiping the air with my fists. "Yup, I went a full three tenths of a mile! This woman was born to run."

That experience sent me to the Word. I wanted to know what the Bible had to say about the subject of *endurance*. Matthew 10:22 talks about enduring to the end, through tribulation and hard times. Hebrews 10:36 says, "For you have need of endurance, so that when you have done the will of God, you may receive what is promised." The Greek word for endurance is derived from a combination of *hyp*, meaning "under," and the verb *meneo*, meaning "to abide." When you are "under" something, you need to "abide" in Him. He'll give you what you need to finish the race.

"Bill, I love what the Lord showed me. This is a principle we can apply to every area of life."

"In the Army, we had to run five miles in the summer heat at Fort Dix, with fifty-pound packs on our backs. It was grueling." Bill shifted in his chair. "I guess you could say this is the Bible version of "no pain, no gain. You have to stay the course, even when you think you're dying."

For nearly a year I jogged faithfully. I didn't understand it at the time, but God had a long-range purpose. There were difficult seasons ahead in my life when I'd need greater strength and endurance. Any time I got bogged down, I'd remember His words to "Lean in. Don't give up, keep going, press into Me."

I often took my running gear with me when I traveled, hoping I'd find time in between meetings to run. During a ministry trip to Ithaca, NY, a few women planned to get together after the retreat and buy my co-worker and myself lunch before we drove home.

Though it was a hot, humid day, after we ate, I decided to jog back to the home where we were staying about three miles away. The last leg of the jog led straight up the infamous Benjamin Hill, one of the steepest hills in Newfield. I'd never driven a hill this steep, much less tried to run it. I asked my travel companion to meet me with the car at the bottom of the hill in half an hour. She agreed, but when I arrived, she was nowhere in sight.

I searched the road for my rescue. The heat pressed down on me. Not even the slightest breeze or hint of shade interrupted the sun's parching rays. Waves of heat radiated up from the black pavement. *Where is she?* Ten minutes went by, twenty. Contemplating the enormous asphalt alpine incline looming in front of me, I had the sudden urge to start running up that hill.

Slow and steady, small *steps, breathe, lean in … anticipate your second wind …* The pavement was too steep. My muscles began to weaken. *You'll never make it. It's impossible, just quit. Look how far it is. Why try? You're no athlete. WHERE IS SHE?* Right in the middle of the steepest part, came the Lord's encouragement.

"Don't look at how far you have to go," He said. "Concentrate on the ground passing beneath your feet." I painstakingly took tiny steps that pushed the pavement past my feet. Slowly, but surely, the last drop of determination squeezed me to a glorious end. I reached the top!

"You're nuts!" I turned to see my friend creep behind me in her car. "Sorry to be so late. Our hostess needed prayer."

"I thought you'd never get here," I sighed, as I flopped into her air-conditioned car. "I worried they'd find me withered up on the side of the road like a prune in jogging shorts. Actually, it's good you didn't come along until now. The Lord spoke to me and gave me another lesson."

Little did I know how many times over the years the Lord would use this simple illustration. He showed me that for the believer the "second wind" is the strengthening of the Holy Spirit. When self-discipline lies far from our reach, or the size of the task seems overwhelmingly difficult, lean in.

My journal entry for the day:

"Today's trip up Benjamin Hill taught me more about drawing on the *barrier-bursting* 'wind' of the Holy Spirit. A woman with all-the-way-through-excellence doesn't give up when things get tough. She presses into Jesus for the strength to finish the impossible mile."

CHAPTER TWENTY-SEVEN

The Wordless Sermon

When I gave my heart to the Lord, I knew absolutely *nothing* about God, Jesus, the Holy Spirit, and the Bible. I couldn't tell you the first thing about what it meant to be "born again." But when the door was opened, God dropped a passion in my heart that turned me into a proverbial sponge to learn everything I could with Bible study and time with the Lord. The more I learned, the stronger that desire grew.

If there was one message I continuously preached in our house, it's that I needed my quiet time with the Lord in order to function. However, with a bustling family, that kind of time became an elusive desire difficult to fulfill.

Our boys were three and five at the time. It wasn't easy to find time alone to study the Bible. I tried reading at the kitchen table, but that proved frustrating. It's not easy to concentrate on Scripture with surround-sound manufactured engine noises and Tonka Trucks crashing all around you. In the winter, my boys rode their Big-Wheels and tricycles *indoors* (I can't believe I said "yes" to that one!). I'd find myself grinding my teeth while reading, "He leadeth me beside still waters..."

For years, my sons insisted on being wherever I was. If I moved to the porch—they'd lug all their toys out there and play at my feet. I couldn't escape. My mother-in-law overheard me complaining about it. "W-e-l-l, Marjorie, "she remarked, "It's none of my b-u-s-i-n-e-s-s, *BUT* you made them love you." (*Oh, why did I have to go and do that?*)

Jeepers, I couldn't even hide in the bathroom for quiet time. Since we only had one bathroom, the moment I slipped into a nice hot tub with my Bible, someone would start banging on the door. "I GOTTA GO!"

I'm sure my mother would cringe if she heard me answer with, "I'm BUSY! Go *OUTSIDE!*"

In the summer, quiet time got drowned out by TV's *Captain Kangaroo* and *Little House on the Prairie*, or endless chauffeuring to play dates, mountains of laundry, gardening, and the constant parade of kids from the neighborhood. Even the dog was in on the conspiracy. He took up residence in my prayer chair.

I tried getting up at 5:00 a.m. to meet with the Lord while the kids and the dog were asleep. No matter how carefully I tip-toed down the hall, the minute my foot hit the top step I'd hear a sleepy, "Mah-omm, are you uh-up?"

"No-ho, I'm na-hot."

"But, we're hungry," whined Jonathan.

I tried throwing them a box of cereal just so they'd stay in bed a little longer. That got my husband's attention. Still glued to his pillow, he contributed, "Bad idea."

Guess who was right? There's nothing as annoying as cleaning up an already cluttered kids' room after a Cheerios fight. No quiet time that day.

When the boys were older, Bill put them to work on the wood pile. Every morning Bill cut and split wood while the boys stacked. This was the perfect time for me to escape to the fields for a quiet time. Our farmhouse sits on 70 acres of land that at one time was known as a thriving strawberry, cantaloupe, and corn farm. Great Grandma Stevens had horses back then and used to graze them on one particular hill that came to be known as the Horse Hill. It was a little oasis, surrounded by lilac bushes and pear trees. I figured the kids would never find me up there, so I hauled a blanket and all my books to that spot and set up camp.

But of course, as soon as Bill determined they'd done enough work for one day, Kyle and Jon invented a new game. "Let's see who can find Mom first!" What a disaster. Since Kyle was older and stronger than Jonathan, he could maneuver through the fields more easily. It was not difficult to know they were on their way with Jon's echoing screams of frustration, "K-Y-L-E...wait for me, NOT FAIR ... K-Y-L-E! ... **MOM!**"

That little oasis was lovely, but sitting on the hard ground got old fast. (Besides, poor Jon was about to blow a gasket.) And it's difficult to concentrate on Scripture with ants crawling up your pant legs. I had to find a new location.

Walking back to the house, I passed Bill's tree stand built about ten feet off the ground in a beautiful maple tree. It even had a little canopy over the top for protection from the rain. *That's it! If it works to camouflage a hunter, maybe it will camouflage me for an hour!*

The screw-in steps leading up the side of the tree were spaced for Bill's 6'4" long legs—an impossible climb for my 5'4" short ones. The next day, while the kids worked with their dad, I dragged an old ladder up to the tree. *Perfect.*

Nobody needed to tell me that ascending a rickety ladder balancing a guitar, a Bible and the Strong's Exhaustive Concordance wasn't a good idea, so I left all that home. Since I didn't own a backpack, I tucked my Bible down my pants, and my journal and pen in my bra and started to climb.

Surprisingly, I scurried up the ladder like a pro (despite my additional cargo). I didn't quite reach the top rung, so I had to really stretch to get my leg in the tree stand. *No one will see me up here.* Sounds of the chainsaw in the distance let me know Bill and the boys were occupied.

This is the perfect spot. The sound of the wind rustling through the leaves carried me away from the stresses of the day. I could feel the sunlight dance across my face as the branches moved in the breeze. I felt the Lord's nearness as I turned my whole heart toward Him. It was glorious until it was time to get down—*WAIT—WHERE'S THE LADDER?!* When I stretched to get on the deer stand, I must have pushed the ladder to the ground!

When you're stuck in a tree where no one can see you or hear you and the family's been conditioned to leave you alone, you're really motivated to pray! It was lunchtime so everyone was inside the house. I yelled for help. Luckily the guy next door was in his yard and heard me. What a relief when I saw him coming over the hill. One look at my dilemma put him in hysterics.

"My ladder fell. It's down there in the weeds. Can you retrieve it for me, please?"

"Maybe I first should ask your husband if he *wants* me to get you down from there?"

"Funny."

"I'm not even going to ask why you're up there," he said, putting the ladder against the tree.

"Can you turn around, please? I don't want you watching this."

He turned around and started home. "This is one for the books," he chuckled. "I can't wait to tell my wife."

The tree stand got written off as an option. *Lord, where can I go now?*

Our used pop-up camper sat in the field. We had purchased it a couple summers ago. It survived three vacations before the canvas began to disintegrate. We should have known you can't buy a camper for $300 and expect much. Now the repairs threatened to cost three times what we'd originally paid for the dumb thing.

"We'll save up and fix it later," Bill said. "Later" never came.

That's it! I'll go in the camper!

At first, it seemed perfect. The ripped canvas let in a nice breeze. There was a table and a padded bench, and I could lock the door! *This is going to be my quiet time place—thank you, Lord.*

I lugged a laundry basket full of research books to the camper, unloaded them, and set out my journal and a box of tissues. I ran back to the house to retrieve my guitar, water, and a snack. Returning, I stuffed a cookie in my mouth and was about to sit down and play my guitar. Out of the corner of my eye I spotted a wasp floating near the window. Just as I was about to hit it with one of my books, I spotted another one—then *another*—and *another*. Soon dozens of wasps emerged from all over the camper. They drifted out from behind the curtains. They hovered around the door, clumsily hitting the glass. Now there were too many wasps between me and the door to escape. The wasps clearly owned the space and I'd better respect them or get stung.

Slowly, I eased myself down on the bench praying that the smell of anxiety emanating from every pore of my body wouldn't arouse their aggression. I took a deep breath, and prayed for protection. *Help me stay calm, Lord.*

Several wasps dropped on the table right in front of me and began crawling across my books. I knew if I tried brushing them away, they'd react. So, I sat stiffly and watched them. Strangely, my heart stopped pounding and I began to have the sense that I was safe. To my surprise, the wasps stopped swarming and began to disappear behind the folds of the curtains. A few lazily drifted past, but not one landed on me.

I decided to stay. The concern about being stung by the wasps subsided, and I was in a quiet place with a nice table, bench, and all my books. God had a lesson in all of this, because nothing happens by accident. Did the Lord want me to be aware that the enemy swarms when a believer seeks to pray? Did He want me to learn about the power of a peaceful heart? It was clear that the wasps calmed down when God helped me relax. I've seen a similar reaction with my kids. When I'm anxious, they become anxious.

When I have anger in my heart, the house becomes chaotic. Even the dog calms down when I'm peaceful.

I opened my journal and wrote a quick note: "I think fear has a smell that attracts the enemy."

My husband thought I was nuts going anywhere near that camper again. But I had the sense I was going to learn a lot being in that very special, quiet, and somewhat dangerous place. "He spreads a table for me in the presence of my enemies" (Psalm 23) I had to hold my peace every time I went in there. It was comical how every time I returned to the camper; the wasps went through the same routine. Emerge—hover—investigate—retreat. Eventually, I got used to them crawling across my books and never once got stung.

The "wasp house" proved sufficient for the bulk of the summer. The boys were learning to respect my prayer and study time. They also showed no interest in coming near those wasps.

 When fall arrived, the boys went back to school and I gravitated inside. The camper reached its last hurrah that winter and had to be carted away, but it was wonderful while it lasted. With the guys gone to school, I had plenty of time alone, but I also had all the household distractions of laundry, dishes, and phone. I read in the Bible, "When you pray, go into your closet and shut the door..." (from Matthew 6:6 KJV). *Why didn't I think of that?*

The only closet in the house big enough and empty enough for a body belonged to Bill. That part of the upstairs hadn't been insulated yet, so it was cold. The big gold bathrobe I'd made Bill hung on a hook against the back wall, so I sat on the floor, and draped it around my shoulders and over my lap so only my head stuck out. I reached for a necktie hanging on the back of the door to pull the door shut. *Perfect!* It was dark and snuggly, a perfect place to pray. All the clothes served as soundproofing. As a matter of fact, it was so quiet I didn't hear Bill come home from work and trudge up the stairs to change his clothes.

When he opened the closet door and saw my head suspended in the middle of a cloud of gold velour, he let out a shriek. Poor Bill jumped a mile, "What are you doing in my closet!" he yelled. "You almost gave me a heart attack."

"S-o-r-r-e-e-e."

"What are you doing in there, anyway?"

"Praying."

I didn't hear what he mumbled under his breath, but I did hear the final dictum, "From now on ... MY closet is OFF LIMITS!"

The Wordless Sermon—More Powerful Than Lecture

As the years passed, the family dynamics changed. The boys didn't play with toys around my feet or climb on my lap anymore. They wanted to be with their friends. I always enjoyed those quiet moments of solitude when I could press into God uninterrupted, but I was learning about the blessing of praying without ceasing. I was learning that prayer didn't always require going away somewhere.

In my early years as a Christian, I had the idea of going "to God" and "from God" instead of seeing that my fellowship is ongoing. My true "prayer closet" is the body I live in, because I am the temple of the Holy Spirit (1 Corinthians 6:19). I can shut the door to the pressures of life while working, and find the company and the strengthening of the Lord without having to change my position. I don't need to have special provisions to enjoy the presence of the Lord.

The passion that started with me personally ended up having a rippling effect on my boys. One day I was kneeling in front of the couch in the living room enveloped in sweet prayer. I heard thirteen-year-old Jon's footsteps behind me. He paused in the doorway and quietly tip-toed away.

Later on, I needed him for something and went to find him. I came around the corner of the living room and there he was, kneeling in the exact position I'd been at the couch. Seeing him follow in my footsteps took my breath away. Jonathan had peeked into my world of prayer, seen my quiet determination to pursue the Lord, and chose to follow. It drove home the truth that children imitate what they see us doing. The example I set as a praying mom was bearing fruit in my children's lives.

In his growing-up years, Jonathan had a difficult time falling asleep. I'd sit at the end of his bed and we'd talk. I think he figured out if he asked me a question about God, I'd get going and stay longer. I'd often talk until he fell asleep. We continued doing this throughout his high school years. I'll never forget the morning he came barreling down the stairs and said, "Hey Mom, you know how I ask you a simple question about God and you go off?"

"Yes, I'm sorry about that, Jon. It's just that I get so excited about the Lord and ..."

"No, Mom, listen—I don't want you to stop!"

Speechless, I watched as he grabbed his jacket and disappeared out the door as the school bus rumbled to a stop at the end of the driveway. *Oh God, he's listening.* A giant tear rolled down my cheek. *Thank you, Lord.*

Life with children is a combination of those gentle talks and wordless sermons we preach to them. I started my walk of intimacy hiding in trees and barricaded in wasp-infested campers. But the Lord showed me that the fruit of quiet time is the *quiet heart* I carry all day long. It's the love language of a worshipful spirit that seals us in His presence every moment of every day.

To the Keeper of My Heart

Marji Stevens

Made in the USA
Monee, IL
17 October 2023

44783887R00118